INTERFET

The Indonesian invasion of the former Portuguese colony of East Timor in 1975 was opposed by a coalition of local nationalist groups who engaged in armed resistance. Many people fled to Australia as refugees. Following years of turmoil and after direct urging from the Howard Government, President BJ Habibie offered the East Timorese self-determination. The United Nations Mission in East Timor (UNAMET) would ensure voting was free and fair. On 30 August 1999, the East Timorese people declared their overwhelming support for independence. Violence initiated by pro-Jakarta militias produced a humanitarian crisis. Xanana Gusmão, former guerrilla leader and independence advocate, called for international military forces to restore order. The UN accepted Australia's offer to lead what became the International Force East Timor (INTERFET) consisting of 22 nations. On 20 September the first elements of the largest Australian deployment since the Vietnam War arrived in the East Timorese capital, Dili. More than 5,500 uniformed men and women were involved in the intervention and many thousands more were to follow over the ensuing three years. On 28 February 2000, INTERFET was dissolved and the United Nations Transitional Administration in East Timor (UNTAET) assumed complete responsibility for peacekeeping operations and civil affairs. The Democratic Republic of Timor-Leste was inaugurated on 20 May 2002.

INTERFET: Lessons and legacies from East Timor 20 years on | Tom Frame (ed.)

ISBN: 9781925826920

Published in 2020 by Connor Court Publishing Pty Ltd

Connor Court Publishing Pty Ltd
PO Box 7257
Redland Bay QLD 4165
sales@connorcourt.com
www.connorcourtpublishing.com.au

Printed in Australia

Cover and page layout by Graham Lindsay

INTERFET

Lessons and legacies from East Timor 20 years on

Edited by **TOM FRAME**

Disclaimer

The views expressed by contributors are their own opinions and do not necessarily represent the position of the Commonwealth of Australia, the University of New South Wales or any organisations with which the contributors were or are now associated. The publication of their chapter in this book does not imply any official agreement or formal concurrence with any opinion, criticism, conclusion or recommendation attributed to them.

CONTENTS

Contributors

General the Honourable Sir Peter Cosgrove AK, CVO, MC

Born into an Army family, Peter Cosgrove attended Waverley College in Sydney before graduating from the Royal Military College, Duntroon, in 1968. His first deployment was in Malaysia with the 1st Battalion RAR and later in South Vietnam where he commanded an infantry platoon. He served as Commander of INTERFET forces in 1999, and was then Chief of Army and later Chief of the Australian Defence Force before becoming a Knight in the Order of Australia (AK) when sworn in as Governor-General in 2014. In retirement, he remains involved with defence, health and other charitable organisations.

Professor Tom Frame AM

Tom Frame joined the RAN College as a cadet midshipman in 1979 and served in the Navy for 15 years. He has been Anglican Bishop to the Australian Defence Force, a Visiting Fellow in the School of Astronomy and Astrophysics at ANU; Patron of the Armed Forces Federation of Australia; a Councillor of the Australian War Memorial and judged the inaugural Prime Minister's Prize for Australian History (2007). He is presently the Director of the Public Leadership Research Group and the Howard Library at UNSW Canberra and is the author or editor of over 50 books.

Dr Martin Hess

In 1979 Martin joined the Australian Army Reserve and served with Melbourne University Regiment, The Far North Queensland Regiment. He joined the Australian Federal Police in 1988. He is a designated detective and has worked in various capacities including investigations, intelligence, surveillance, close personal protection and general duties throughout Australia. Martin has deployed internationally with the AFP on a number of occasions: UNFICYP (Cyprus 1996) UNAMET (East Timor 1999) Afghanistan–AFP Op Illuminate (2010–11). His academic qualifications include a Master of Defence Studies, a Master of Leadership and Management, a PhD on Australian international policing at the Australian National University. Martin has recently engaged in some casual university tutoring positions in Canberra related to criminology and Australian security in the Asian century. He presently works for the International Operations portfolio of the AFP. Between 2014–2016 he worked as the police adviser to the Australian Civil Military Centre in Queanbeyan, NSW, before transferring a role as an AFP Liaison Officer to the ADF Joint Operations Command Headquarters, where he works collaboratively with all three services in various capacities, dealing primarily with ongoing AFP investigations and major event planning.

The Honourable John Howard OM, AC

John Howard was the twenty-fifth Prime Minister of Australia, leading the nation from March 1996 to December 2007. He was the federal member for Bennelong in the House of Representatives (1974–2007) and filled several ministerial and shadow ministerial posts prior to 1996. He was made a Companion of the Order of Australia (AC) and appointed to the Order of Merit (OM) in 2012. He is the second-longest serving prime minister of Australia.

Professor David Kilcullen

David Kilcullen is an Australian author, strategist and counterinsurgency expert and is currently the non-executive Chairman and a Founder of Caerus Associates, a strategy and design consulting firm. Building on his experience as a strategist and soldier, he was motivated by the idea that conflict is dynamic and hyper-local. David served for 25 years as a light infantry officer in the Australian Army. He is now considered one of the world's leading experts on guerrilla warfare. He has served in every theatre of the 'War on Terror' since 9/11, as special advisor for counter-insurgency to Secretary of State Condoleezza Rice, senior counter-insurgency advisor to General David Petraeus in Iraq, and chief counter-terrorism strategist for the US State Department. He is a former Australian Army officer with combat experience in South-East Asia and the Middle East. He completed a Bachelor of Arts with Honours in Military Art and Science at UNSW. In 1993, David graduated from the Australian Defence Force School of Languages with an Advanced Diploma in Applied Linguistics. He is fluent in Indonesian and speaks some Arabic and French. He received a PhD in politics from the UNSW in 2000 and now teaches at UNSW Canberra.

Air Vice-Marshal Kym Osley AM, CSC

Kym has 42-years service in the RAAF with the last five years in the Reserve. He flew as an Air Combat Officer in fast jets (primarily F-111 and Phantoms), including as Officer Commanding 82 Wing and Commander of Air Combat Group. In 2006–07, Kym directed the efforts of 25,000 Coalition airmen employing over 400 aircraft supporting military operations in Afghanistan and Iraq. As Commanding Officer of No 1 Squadron, he led the F-111 reconnaissance operations over East Timor in 1999. His postings at senior level have included Head of Australian Defence Staff (Washington), Air Adviser to the United Kingdom, and Program Manager for the Australian F-35 Program. In addition to his Reserve roles as Chair of the

Air Cadet Foundation and supporting Defence Industry, he is also a Managing Director in the Canberra Office of PricewaterhouseCoopers.

Dr Alan Ryan

Alan Ryan is Executive Director of the Australian Civil-Military Centre, preparing Australian capability for conflicts and disasters overseas. He has served as: the Principal of the Centre for Defence and Strategic Studies at the Australian Defence College; the Strategic Adviser to the Minister for Defence; Senior Research Fellow in the Land Warfare Studies Centre; and Assistant Dean at the University of Notre Dame Australia. He conducted the ADF lessons analysis for INTERFET. He has a PhD from Cambridge University and a BA (Hons) and Law degree from the University of Melbourne. He has published over 40 books, chapters and articles.

Commodore Jim Stapleton AM

Jim Stapleton joined the Naval College Jervis Bay in 1969 and subsequently served in the Royal Australian Navy for 36 years. He qualified as an above Water Warfare Officer in the UK in 1978 and following exchange service with the Royal Navy returned to Fleet headquarters Sydney. Jim had a predominantly operational career including several sea commands and Director of the Naval Warfare School at HMAS WATSON. Following the Australian Defence College he took up a posting as Commodore Flotillas in Maritime Command which included a period as the INTERFET Naval Component Commander in East Timor. Jim completed his career as Naval Attaché Washington, DC during the second Gulf war.

Professor Craig Stockings

Craig Stockings is the Official Historian of Australian Operations in Iraq, Afghanistan and East Timor. Craig is a graduate of both the Australian Defence Force Academy, and the Royal Military College, Duntroon. As an infantry officer he served in a range of regimental appointments within the 3rd Battalion, Royal Australian Regiment. As a junior officer he served during the INTERFET deployment to East Timor in 1999–2000, followed by an appointment as the Aide-de-Camp to the Governor-General of the Commonwealth of Australia. Craig holds a First Class Honours Degree in History, Masters qualifications in International Relations and Education, and a PhD in History. Prior to his appointment as Official Historian, Craig was a Professor of History at the University of New South Wales (Canberra). His areas of academic interest concern general and Australian military history and operational analysis. He has published a wide range of scholarly articles, book chapters and books in the field. Most notably these include a history of the army cadet movement in Australia entitled: *The Torch and the Sword,* a study of the First Libyan Campaign in North Africa 1940- 41: *Bardia: Myth, Reality and the Heirs of Anzac,* a re-interpretation of the German invasion of Greece in 1941 entitled: *Swastika over the Acropolis* (with Associate Professor Eleanor Hancock), and most recently: *Britannia's Shield: Lieutenant-General Sir Edward Hutton and Late Victorian Imperial Defence.* He has also edited a number of books including *Zombie Myths of Australian Military History, Anzac's Dirty Dozen: 12 Myths of Australian Military History,* Before the Anzac Dawn (with Dr John Connor), and a forthcoming work entitled: *The Shadow Men: the leaders who shaped the Australian Army from the Veldt to Vietnam.*

Major General Paul Symon AO

Paul Symon graduated from the Royal Military College Duntroon in 1982. A career in the military, spanning 35 years and culminating in the rank of Major General, followed. From 2011–14, Paul was Director of the Defence Intelligence Organisation and, prior to that, served as the Deputy Chief of the Australian Army from late 2008 until 2011. Paul has served on operations four times during his military career. His most senior command was as a Brigadier in late 2005 until mid-2006 when he was appointed Australian Commander Middle East. This gave him national command responsibility for all Defence personnel in Iraq and Afghanistan. Prior to that appointment, in 2003, he was selected to be the senior military adviser to Nick Warner the Special Coordinator of the Regional Assistance Mission in the Solomon Islands (RAMSI). In 1999, Paul was the Australian senior military officer in East Timor during the months preceding the ballot for East Timor's independence. His team of five officers found themselves negotiating with militia and Falantil leaders, as well as the United Nations (UN) and Indonesian military, to deliver a ballot to the people of East Timor during a period of high tension and duress. He was made a Member of the Order of Australia (AM) for his service in East Timor. Prior to that, in 1997, he served with the United Nations in Southern Lebanon and on the Golan Heights. Paul is the 1982 recipient of the Sword of Honour and Blamey Award at Duntroon. He holds two Master's degrees: from the University of New South Wales and from Deakin University. He was also appointed an Officer of the Order of Australia (AO). In mid-2015, Paul left the military and joined the Department of Foreign Affairs and Trade. He was subsequently appointed Director General of the Australian Secret Intelligence Service from 18 December 2017.

Michael Ward

Michael Ward graduated from the Royal Military College in 1984 and served in a variety or regimental and staff appointments during a 20-year Army career.

After leaving the military, Michael served in several executive roles in Raytheon Australia before taking on the position of Managing Director in 2009 where he has since grown the business to become one of the country's largest and most capable defence companies. Michael has been as an active participant on numerous bodies including the Air Warfare Destroyer Principals' Council, the Submarine Enterprise Board and the Prime Minister's Industry Advisory Committee on Veterans Employment.

The Honourable Penny Wensley AC

Penny Wensley was Governor of Queensland from 2008–14. Her appointment followed a distinguished career as a diplomat (1968–2008), representing Australia in a wide range of bilateral and multilateral postings overseas and senior policy positions in Canberra. After early postings to France, Mexico, and New Zealand, she served successively as Consul-General, Hong Kong; Ambassador to the UN, Geneva; Ambassador for the Environment, Ambassador to the UN, New York; High Commissioner to India; and Ambassador to France. In Canberra, she headed the East Asia Branch, International Organisations and Legal Division, North Asia Division, and Europe Division. Penny has a Bachelor of Arts (First Class Honours) degree from the University of Queensland (UQ) and Honorary Doctorates from UQ, James Cook and Griffith universities, and the Queensland University of Technology. She is a Fellow of the Australian Institute of International Affairs (FAIIA) and an Honorary Fellow of the Environment Institute of Australia and New Zealand (HFEANZ). She is currently Chairman of the Council of the Australian Institute of Marine Science (AIMS), Chairman of the Reef 2050 Advisory Committee, and Board Director of the Lowy Institute. She was made an offficer of the Order of Australia (AO) in 2001 for distinguished contributions to international relations and a Companion of the Order (AC), *inter alia*, as a key contributor to the initiatives of the United Nations.

INTERFET TIMELINE

Trish Burgess

1998

21 May 1998   Dr BJ Habibie takes the oath of office as President of Indonesia.

19 December 1998   John Howard, Prime Minister of Australia since March 1996, writes to President Habibie advising of an Australian foreign policy change to support a period of autonomy in East Timor followed by an act of self-determination.

1999

27 January   President Habibie issues a public statement that his Government might be prepared to consider independence for East Timor.

11 March   Tripartite talks in New York reach agreement on a direct ballot of the East Timor's people - to accept or reject an autonomy proposal.

February-April   Independence Leader Xanana Gusmao moved from an Indonesian prison to house arrest. After increasing violence by anti-independence activists, Gusmao encourages resumption of the independence struggle.

5 May   Agreement between the governments of Indonesia and Portugal allows for the United Nations (UN) to organise and conduct a vote of the East Timorese to accept or reject special autonomy status within the Republic of Indonesia.

11 June	The UN Security Council formally establishes the United Nations Mission in East Timor (UNAMET): 'The Council stresses again the responsibility of the Indonesian Government in the maintenance of peace and security in East Timor to ensure the integrity of the ballot and the security of international staff and observers'.
18 June	The Special Representative of the UN Secretary-General, Ian Martin, observes that 'continuing violence has forced tens of thousands of East Timorese from their homes creating a 'serious obstacle' to preparations for the vote'.
23 June	UN Secretary-General Kofi Annan announces that, due to continuing violence and logistical problems, there will be a two-week delay (to 13 July) in commencing the registration and voting procedure.
16 July	Voter registration begins.
5 August	Voter registration closes. UNAMET registered 451 792 potential voters (of population of over 800 000 in East Timor and abroad).
August	Frequent reports of violence, intimidation and additional security during campaigning. East Timorese leaders from pro-independence and pro-autonomy groups agree to establish a 25-person commission to foster cooperation and reconciliation until the results of the ballot are implemented.
30 August	Voting takes place after a delay of nearly two weeks.
4 September	UNAMET announces the result: 94 388 or 21.5 percent of East Timorese voted in favor of the special autonomy proposal and 344 580 or 78.5 percent voted against. A total of 446 953 or 96.6 percent of registered East Timorese cast their ballots within and beyond the territory.
	Following the result there is more violence by anti-independence militia and Indonesian military with estimates of up to 1000 people killed. Villages are burned and infrastructure destroyed. A quarter of the population flees, mainly to West Timor.
7 September	Independence leader, Xanana Gusmao, freed from house arrest.

10 September	Lawlessness increases and militia members threaten to invade the UN compound in Dili. The UN Secretary-General urges the Indonesian Government to accept offers of assistance to restore order from several governments including Australia, New Zealand, the Philippines and Malaysia.
15 September	The Government of Indonesia agrees to accept the offer of assistance from the international community. The Security Council authorises a multinational force (INTERFET).
	The United Nations begins a large-scale emergency humanitarian relief effort. At the same time, increasing attention is paid to the voluntary repatriation of some 250 000 East Timorese from West Timor and other areas in Indonesia and the region.
20 September	First INTERFET troops arrive in Dili under the command of Australian Major General Peter Cosgrove. Demonstrations are held outside the Australian Embassy in Jakarta by Indonesians angry at Australia's role in peace keeping. Order is slowly restored in East Timor with many militia fleeing to West Timor. The main Australian combat element included infantry and cavalry that was provided by the Australian Army's 3rd Brigade.
29 September	The first New Zealand infantry arrive. With the city of Dili secured, INTERFET personnel begin moving into rural towns and villages.
1 October	Australian forces secure Balibo and Batugade near the western border. Maliana is then secured before clearing militia from the remainder of the Bobonaro Regency.

16 October	A major contact occurs at Aidabasalala, a town 15 kilometres (9.3 miles) from the West Timor border. During the action, involving an Australian covert reconnaissance patrol from the SASR, the Australians were repeatedly attacked in a series of fire-fights by more than 20 militia. The SASR patrol had been detected while establishing an observation post and were forced to fight their way to a landing zone, being attacked on a further three occasions over a 90 minute period, killing a number of their attackers before they were successfully extracted by Black Hawk helicopter. Five militia were killed and three wounded. There were no Australian casualties.
18 October	The Indonesian Parliament endorses the referendum result and declares void the 1976 annexation of East Timor.
25 October	The United Nations Transitional Administration in East Timor (UNTAET) is established to guide the territory towards independence.
1 November	The last Indonesian troops depart East Timor.
1 December	José Ramos Horta, founder of Fretilin and international spokesman for the East Timorese resistance, returns to East Timor after an exile of 24 years. He was co-recipient of the 1996 Nobel Peace Prize.

2002

20 May	UNTAET ends and the Democratic Republic of East Timor becomes an independent nation recognised by the United Nations.

ABBREVIATIONS AND ACRONYMS

ABC	Australian Broadcasting Corporation
ADF	Australian Defence Force
AEC	Australian Electoral Commission
AFP	Australian Federal Police
ASEAN	Association of South East Asian Nations
IDG	International Deployment Group (AFP)
INP	Indonesian National Police (see also POLRI)
INTERFET	International Force for East Timor
IO	International Operations (AFP)
PTCN	Pacific Transnational Crime Network
PNTL	*Policia Nacionale Timor Leste*
POLRI	Police of the Republic of Indonesia
RAAF	Royal Australian Air Force
RAN	Royal Australian Navy
RAMSI	Regional Assistance Mission to the Solomon Islands
RMC	Royal Military College (Duntroon)
SIPDP	Solomon Islands Police Development Program
SRSG	Special Representative of the Secretary General (UN)
TLPDP	Timor Leste Police Development Program
TNI	*Tentara Nasional Indonesia* (Indonesian military)
UNAMET	United Nations Mission East Timor
UNTAET	United Nations Transitional Authority East Timor
UNMISET	United Nations Mission of Support to East Timor
UNMIT	United Nations Integrated Mission in Timor-Leste

INTRODUCTION

Tom Frame

The first 40 years of my life were dominated by two long-running and seemingly intractable conflicts. As one finished, the other started. Shortly before I was born in October 1962, the Menzies Government dispatched the Australian Army Training Team to Vietnam. Their role was to mentor the South Vietnamese army which was opposing a rapidly escalating communist insurgency sponsored by North Vietnam. The insurgency's aim was a single and united Vietnamese state ruled from Hanoi. In April 1965, Australia committed a combat battalion to South Vietnam and gradually escalated its involvement to include ships and aircraft. At its peak strength in 1968–69, over 7600 Australians were deployed to the multi-national taskforce that was attempting to prevent the politically unstable South Vietnam from being overrun. Until 1968, the majority of Australians supported the war and its objectives, fearing the expansion of communist influence in the region to the north of the continent. Perhaps surprisingly, there was also widespread community endorsement for national service (conscription) which came with the prospect of being sent overseas for potentially hazardous service.

Australia's involvement in the war in Vietnam was the most controversial military deployment in the nation's history. Public protests and civil disobedience symbolised the growing tide of opposition. I can recall from my childhood Anzac Day marches being interrupted by protesters chanting slogans I did not then understand. These were deeply unsettling experiences for a young person. My father's trade union, the Federated Engine Drivers' and Firemen's Association (FEDFA), was divided over whether its opposition to the war should frustrate the handling of Australian supply ships bound for Vung Tau, a port on the south-eastern coastline of South Vietnam that served Phuoc Tuy province where Australian forces were based. Although Australian ground forces were gradually withdrawn during 1971–72, and naval and air elements the following year, it was not until April 1975 that the war formally ended with the collapse of the Saigon Government and reunification of the entire country. The war had sapped the political will of successive Australian governments and prompted anti-military sentiment in many sections of the population, especially within families whose young men were conscripted. This was the first armed conflict in which Australia had not been on the victorious side. Much bitterness remained among those who deployed and those who deplored the conduct of the war. As I bring to mind television news images of the last military helicopter departing from the United States Embassy in Saigon, I recognise the war certainly influenced my rapidly evolving sense of world affairs and my impressions of uniformed service ahead of joining the Royal Australian Navy a few years later.

Several months after a detachment of North Vietnamese tanks had broken through the front gates of the presidential palace in Saigon, Indonesian forces began to prepare for an invasion of the small Portuguese colony of East Timor. Few Australians knew much about East Timor before 1975 and even fewer cared that it was among the few remaining European colonies in the region; the others being the condominium of the New Hebrides (now Vanuatu), the Solomon Islands, and the Gilbert and Ellice Islands (now Kiribati and Tuvalu). Australia granted independence to the Territory of Papua New Guinea on 16 September 1975.

As a first year high school student I knew nothing of the history of East Timor or its imminent struggles despite its nearness to Australia. It did not feature in any of the subjects I was studying nor attract any attention in our current affairs classes. Anzac Day orations sometimes mentioned the Australian military personnel who had worked with their British and Dutch counterparts to oppose Japan's occupation of Timor in 1942–43. Much of East Timor's past was simply unknown. Proclaimed a Portuguese settlement in 1679, the eastern half of the island had been ruled by Lisbon for three centuries. The western half (with the exclusion of a small enclave around the coastal settlement of Oecussi-Ambeno) was administered by the Dutch and became part of the newly-formed Republic of Indonesia in 1949. As other European nations agreed, or were coerced, into granting independence to their colonies, Portugal tried to retain possession of Guinea, Angola, Mozambique and Macau. Antonio de Oliveira Salazar, the leader of Portugal's one-party state after 1933, was firmly committed to a 'pluricontinental' Portugal—a single political entity spread across several territories. Its colonies were considered overseas provinces. After the 1974 'Carnation Revolution' opened the country to democracy and liberalism, Portugal prepared to relinquish its last remaining colony and its most distant one, East Timor. With little time to prepare effectively for transition to nationhood, East Timor's rival political factions turned on each other in their quest for supremacy. Fearing a possible descent into political chaos and social disintegration, and unwilling to countenance the possibility of a communist regime on its doorstep, the President of Indonesia, General Suharto, ordered the occupation of East Timor in December 1975 ahead of its incorporation into the Republic of Indonesia as the country's 27th province in July 1976.

The prelude to the invasion and the invasion itself were poorly reported in Australia which was preoccupied with its own political struggles. Evidence of the infiltration of East Timor by Indonesian agents was, however, being slowly uncovered and steadily conveyed to the Australian people. Five journalists (two Australians, two Britons and one New Zealander) working for Australian media networks—who became known as the 'Balibo Five'—were covering developments along the West Timor border. Unarmed, dressed in civilian clothes and clearly identifying themselves as representatives of Australian media, they were murdered by the Indonesian military on 16 October 1975 to minimise the flow of news and the supply of images. Another journalist, Roger East, travelled to Balibo after hearing that the newsmen had been killed and was executed in Dili by the Indonesian military on 8 December 1975. By then, the East Timorese independence party, Fretilin, had issued a declaration of independence from Portugal. It was a symbolic gesture that lacked any practical substance.

I recall watching television reports on the conflict and chaos that gripped East Timor in the second half of 1975, and allegations that the Indonesian military was behind the internal unrest that it fully intended to exploit as justification for the invasion. Most Australians aware of world events at that time can remember seeing pictures of a small house in Balibo town square with one wall bearing a hand-painted national flag with the word

'AUSTRALIA' emblazoned above it. The Indonesian claim that the reporters and their cameramen were caught in crossfire was considered ludicrous. It was actually an admission of Indonesian guilt. As a politically left-leaning teenager with strong opinions on most subjects, I was adamant that the Indonesians responsible for the deaths of the 'Balibo Five' ought to be tried for murder and other war crimes. Although I had not previously thought about East Timor, like many Australians, I had become an energetic advocate for the liberation and freedom of its people.

Claims that Australia was complicit in the invasion were deeply distressing. The Whitlam Government, whose commission had been terminated by Governor-General Sir John Kerr on 11 November 1975, had done nothing to inhibit the Indonesians during the previous months. It intended to accept the invasion and acknowledge the political reunification of the island. The caretaker government led by Malcolm Fraser was preoccupied with the election campaign that brought it to office. It was constrained from making any major decisions. Australians went to the polls on 13 December 1975. By then, the Indonesians had invaded East Timor, deployed 35 000 troops, expelled the recently formed Fretilin government from Dili, defeated a small force of Falintil fighters (who were aligned with Fretilin) and established an Interim Government. Within a few weeks, part of Portugal had become part of Indonesia.

In reality, there was little if anything that Canberra could have done practically or politically to prevent the invasion. There was no appetite within Australia for any form of military intervention so soon after the end of the Vietnam Conflict. Within the Labor Government, a persuasive body of opinion held that the best interests of the East Timorese and the region would not be served by supporting an act of self-determination and then, very likely, independent nationhood. Prime Minister Whitlam apparently believed the division of Timor was no more than an accident of European colonial history that ought to be remedied. Nor was he prepared to support any of the nascent separatist movements in Indonesia, preferring to avoid the prospect of dividing what was already an ethnically and socially disparate nation. Gareth Evans, the Minister for Foreign Affairs in the Hawke and Keating governments (1988–96), claimed that no-one could have predicted that the 1975 invasion would be followed by years of brutal oppression and widespread disregard for human rights. Other observers thought differently, pointing to the conduct of the Indonesian military in West Timor and West Papua (previously Dutch New Guinea) as evidence that it often acted beyond any legal restraint.

As in South Vietnam, the attitude and actions of the Australian Government were the source of domestic political controversy. During the 1960s the claim was often made that the citizens of South Vietnam had chosen to live in a non-communist society and were entitled to determine their own future free from intimidation from the agents of the communist regime in Hanoi. Their democratic decision needed to be respected and, if necessary, upheld by force. This was the rhetorical basis for Australia's involvement in Vietnam's long-running civil war notwithstanding the incompetence and corruption that depleted the confidence of South Vietnam's international supporters, including Australia. In 1975, there was little doubt that the majority of East Timorese did not want to live as citizens of Indonesia. Very few had shown support for the Timorese Popular Democratic Association, also known as APODETI. Formed in 1974, its leaders felt East Timor could not survive as an independent nation and needed to become part of Indonesia. Although it promoted 'autonomous integration', APODETI could not compete with the more popular independence parties. After the Indonesian invasion, the democratic desires of the local people did not seem to matter. Their political will could be overlooked if the national interests of Australia and Indonesia deemed it necessary.

Despite international denunciations of the invasion, opposition to its subsequent annexation, and the insistence of the United Nations' Security Council that East Timor was a 'non-self-governing territory under Portuguese administration', the actions of the Indonesian military in 1975–76 were validated, if not legitimated, by a succession of Australian governments in their dealings with the Suharto regime over the next two decades. This attitude was maintained despite clear evidence that the Indonesian military was conducting campaigns of violent intimidation and systematic brutality against what remained of East Timor's independence movement. In 1991, the massacre of more than 250 civilians in Santa Cruz cemetery after a funeral was secretly filmed and then widely distributed. The Hawke Labor Government was subsequently condemned for preserving its treaty with Indonesia for the joint exploration of oil and gas fields adjacent to East Timor. The Keating Government, which prided itself on a close and constructive relationship with the Suharto regime, was chastised for refusing to grant political asylum to those fleeing persecution in the troubled province.

Rather ironically, the Australian Government was criticised for what it did in South Vietnam and castigated for what it did not do in East Timor. In 1991, while still a serving naval officer, I was formally censured for publishing an article in the *Canberra Times* that lamented the hypocrisy of the Australian Government in responding immediately to the Iraqi invasion of Kuwait in August 1990 while refusing to condemn the Indonesian occupation of East Timor 15 years earlier. As more and more Australians became aware of how oppressive the Indonesian occupation remained, and as independence advocates like Jose Ramos Horta, who was based in Melbourne and gathered a considerable support base, were able to raise the profile of East Timorese suffering, the plight of the former Portuguese colony was never far from sight. Realising the deep feelings of the Australian public, Suharto avoided visiting Australia and providing opportunities for independence advocates to draw global attention to their cause. Meanwhile, the United Nations adopted no fewer than 10 resolutions condemning the invasion and annexation, as details of Indonesian atrocities on the island continued to emerge despite determined efforts by the security forces to isolate the province from the gaze of the media.

After it won office in March 1996, the Howard Government persisted with Labor's policy on East Timor. The Coalition's policy platform did not include any concessions to East Timorese independence, believing that a close and constructive relationship with the long-standing Suharto regime was very much in Australia's national interests. It assiduously avoided commenting on Indonesian internal affairs including the suppression of pro-democracy movements. Deputy Prime Minister and Trade Minister, Tim Fischer, described Suharto as one of the greatest world leaders of the late twentieth century. It was not a view shared by an informed Australian public that felt uncomfortable with, if not hostile to, what they saw as the continuing complicity of the Australian Government in the sufferings of the East Timorese.

The available options were few although the Howard Government was much less anxious about annoying Indonesia than its predecessors. Would the Coalition now condemn what previous Australian governments had condoned? Could it persuade the Indonesian Government to take a different approach to East Timor or, at least, restrain the worst excesses of its military forces deployed there? Was there scope to secure a diplomatic solution that would not harm the relationship between Australia and Indonesia more generally? Were sanctions or the suspension of aid and assistance a possible solution? The use of force would have been tantamount to an invasion and was never seriously considered. As Australia had accepted East Timor's incorporation into the Indonesian republic and had subsequently acted in a manner that acknowledged Indonesian sovereignty over the territory, any direct action on Australia's part would have been cast as intolerable interference in the internal affairs of its neighbour. After a regional economic crisis brought Indonesia's financial system to the verge of collapse and led to the resignation of President Suharto in May 1998, the Howard Government was presented with a significant opportunity to encourage reform within Indonesia and rethinking within Australia. Canberra's position shifted very quickly from one of disapproving resistance towards East Timorese self-determination to encouraging its autonomy within the Indonesian republic. This collection of essays is about the events—expected and unexpected—that flowed from the change in Australia's policy in 1998.

Each of the contributors to this collection was personally involved in the East Timor 'crisis' of 1998–2000. John Howard was the Prime Minister of Australia; Penny Wensley was Australia's Ambassador and Permanent Representative to the United Nations in New York; Michael Ward was part of the secretariat supporting the Joint Parliamentary Committee on Foreign Affairs, Defence and Trade; Paul Symon headed the Australian military component of the United Nations Mission in East Timor (UNAMET); Martin Hess was attached to UNAMET's civilian police contingent; Peter Cosgrove commanded the international intervention force in East Timor; Jim Stapleton was the naval commander in East Timor; David Kilcullen was an infantry officer whose unit came under fire near the Indonesian border; Kim Osley was a senior pilot who flew reconnaissance missions over East Timor; Alan Ryan was involved in inter-departmental liaison teams in Canberra; and, Craig Stockings was part of the first infantry battalion sent to restore order in what remained *de facto* Indonesian territory until 31 October 1999 and *de jure* Indonesian Territory until 20 May 2002. [I visited East Timor in November-December 2001 as Anglican Bishop to the Australian Defence Force.]

Each contributor was asked to write from a personal and professional perspective about what they observed of Australia's response to the crisis, drawing the attention of readers to what went well and, perhaps less widely known, what went wrong. They were also asked to settle on a small number of lessons that were learned from UNAMET and the International Force East Timor (INTERFET) that led to specific innovation or general reforms. Each was invited to end with a reflection on what readers should make of the enduring legacies of this tumultuous period. It marked a turning point in the careers of most contributors and defined a high point in their service to the nation.

As editor, I asked them to mindful of two hazards. The first is writing in a self-interested way. The second is overlooking individual preference or institutional bias. These are reasonable concerns given the human desire to embellish the past and the tendency to overlook failures. After reflecting on the chapters in this collection, it is clear that a connection with the events of 1999 has assisted each contributor to make greater sense of what occurred. Many have drawn on personal experiences and familiarity with the people and the pressures that have shaped the contemporary Australian Defence Force (ADF), the Australian Federal Police (AFP) and the Australian Public Service (APS). They were encouraged to be candid in expressing their personal opinions while recognising the essentiality of maintaining professional detachment.

The first drafts of these chapters were presented at a symposium held on 17 September 2019 at Defence headquarters in Canberra to coincide with the 20th anniversary of the INTERFET deployment. The symposium was hosted by the UNSW Canberra Public Leadership Research Group and generously sponsored by Raytheon Australia. The Ambassador of Timor-Leste to Australia, Mr Abel Guterres, was interviewed on his experiences of Portuguese colonial rule, the Indonesian invasion, his escape from Bacau to Australia in 1975, the death of his siblings during the Indonesian occupation and how the 1999 crisis is presented to a rising generation of young East Timorese. A video of the interview is available on Youtube.

Much has happened since 1999 as a consequence of the UNAMET and INTERFET deployments and many lessons are still to be applied. In the case of deep-seated cultural deficiencies, the causes and consequences of an organisational mindset might not be apparent for decades. There is a continuing need to be better informed about government activities and achievements while gaining a deeper appreciation of the tests of leadership in politics and diplomacy, strategy and tactics, organisation and logistics, military intelligence and public information, human performance and ethical direction. More broadly, this collection should prompt discussion and provoke debate about what the ADF, the AFP and the APS can glean from its recent experiences and how that learning should be absorbed into their activities both now and into the future. Many questions are still to be asked of the UNAMET and INTERFET deployments. This collection will encourage thinking not only about the answers but whether the right questions are really being asked. There is no better time for such an activity than the present.

Tom Frame
Howard Library
Old Parliament House
Canberra, ACT
April 2020

CHAPTER 1

A political perspective

John Howard

F or many years East Timor had been on the collective conscience of Australians. In the lead up to 1999 one felt that in some way things had to be put right with East Timor. There was a remarkable coincidence of groups within the Australian community, not normally in alignment on political and strategic issues, who felt great sympathy and sentiment towards the people of East Timor. Those who had been connected in any way to the Second World War, particularly those who had been captured by the Japanese in East Timor, remembered with great affection the support they received from the East Timorese people. My close friend, political mentor and parliamentary colleague, the late Sir John Carrick, deployed to Timor in 1942 as part of 'Sparrow Force' and was captured and imprisoned by the Japanese. He always spoke highly of local resistance to the Japanese occupation.

In a political context, the Australian Labor Party, which was in government for a very long period between the incorporation of East Timor into Indonesia in July 1976 and the deployment of the Australian-led INTERFET in September 1999, was deeply divided. The Labor Left was never happy with how the Whitlam Government handled the Indonesian invasion in December 1975. Nor had they ever warmed to President Suharto. Their feeling was that during his rise to power in the mid-1960s there had been savage reprisals against his political opponents, particularly the Chinese population, and his conduct ought to be condemned. There was also a religious context. Because of the Portuguese provenance of East Timor, the Catholic Church was very strong in advocating a fairer deal for the predominantly Christian community who found themselves forcibly incorporated into the world's largest Muslim nation as its 27th province.

There was growing discomfort across the political divide that Australia was complicit in the incorporation of East Timor into the Indonesian republic. It is important for me, as a Coalition Prime Minister of Australia, to acknowledge this bipartisan acquiescence and the role of my party in its perpetuation. Any suggestion of a clear political divide from 1975 until 1999 is simply mistaken. In the dying months of the Whitlam Government and as a member of the Fraser Government, I recall decisions being taken that effectively confirmed the *de facto* acceptance of East Timor's fate. It was a bipartisan policy that was supported by successive Australian governments which found it in their interests to recognise the sovereignty of Indonesia over East Timor. As time went by, attitudes began to change especially as stories emerged of routine intimidation and systematic oppression.

When I became Prime Minister in March 1996, the prevailing view in diplomatic circles in Canberra was that we should not upset Jakarta. The well-entrenched orthodoxy was that having good relations with Indonesia was the *sine qua non* of good Australian foreign policy. This was the dominant stream of advice coming formally to the government from both the Department of Foreign Affairs and Trade as well as the Department of the Prime Minister and Cabinet. It was built on the quite legitimate view that Indonesia was our nearest neighbour, as well as the largest Muslim nation in the world, with whom Australia had a regularly difficult relationship. I am not suggesting that it was only because of the advice that the Government received that the Coalition parties adopted the policy. It was the policy widely embraced throughout those years and it was certainly the policy that the Coalition endorsed in the election campaign of February-March 1996.

I remember well my first official visit to Jakarta in September 1996. It was also my first overseas trip after becoming Prime Minister. I was met at the airport by the Foreign Minister of Indonesia, Ali Alatas. We talked about the more sensitive issues that I might discuss with President Suharto. We also talked about East Timor, specifically how much time we wanted to spend talking about its future. There had been a number of worrying incidents that could not be wished out of existence and I felt obliged to raise them. I was thinking mainly of the 'Balibo Five', five journalists, two of them Australian, who covering the prelude to the Indonesian invasion in December 1975, who were killed in October 1975; and also the shooting of more than 250 pro-independence demonstrators in the Santa Cruz cemetery in November 1991. I told Alatas that I would be raising Australia's concerns about the behaviour of Indonesia-backed militias and the conduct of the Indonesian army, the TNI, in East Timor.

Until 1999, the conventional wisdom was that the Australian Government ought to define its engagement with Asia by the quality of its relations with Jakarta. In a political sense, the big change occurred when President Suharto was forced to resign the presidency as a consequence of the 1997 Asian financial crisis. As a result, Dr BJ Habibie became the President of Indonesia in May 1998. It was a remarkable transfer of power. My government welcomed Habibie's elevation from the vice-presidency. He was different from Suharto. In fact, he was about as different as anyone could imagine and in every respect. He did not have a background in the military and had spent a large part of the previous 20 years of his life living and working abroad as a senior executive of the Messerschmitt corporation.

Habibie regarded East Timor as a burden for Indonesia and brought a fresh attitude to its future. Put simply, he did not think East Timor was worth the trouble it was causing Indonesia at home or abroad. Further, worrying about East Timor would not rank very highly on his agenda for the country. This was not the thinking of many in the Indonesian military, particularly President Habibie's Defence Minister, General Wiranto. Plainly, Habibie did not share the commitment and involvement of the Indonesian military in retaining East Timor as part of Indonesia. The Indonesian military had fought a number of battles and lost many of its personnel in East Timor. The new President seemed to be an Indonesian leader who might look again at the relationship between the Republic of Indonesia and its unruly 27th province. I felt this was a unique opportunity to seize the moment and achieve an outcome that served the needs of Indonesia and Australia.

I was also conscious that international opinion had begun to move. In 1998, not long after the October federal election in Australia, we had a meeting of the National Security Committee of Cabinet. Alexander Downer, on the urging of the Secretary of the Department of Foreign Affairs and Trade,

Ashton Calvert, outlined what he perceived to be shifts in the attitudes of the key stakeholders to East Timor and its future. In sum, Australia needed to consider changing its policy to avoid being left behind.

This productive discussion prompted me to write to President Habibie towards the end of 1999. The message I wanted to convey on behalf the Australian Government was that the circumstances in East Timor had changed and the time had come to give the people of East Timor an opportunity to express a view about their future. Notably, my letter did not recommend or even canvas full independence. It suggested a series of alternatives well short of offering the prospect of nationhood to East Timor. One of the alternatives was giving East Timor much greater autonomy within the Indonesian Republic.

To our surprise, not only did Habibie agree that a new approach was needed, he went much further than we ever imagined. Quite significantly, Habibie decided to give expression to his own feelings in deciding to offer the East Timorese full independence if that was their desire. What the letter exposed was a sharp difference of opinion within the Indonesian establishment. Habibie was not alone in his attitude to East Timor but there were many within but also beyond the military who thought differently and disagreed with his stance. Our surprise continued when he decided that the future of East Timor needed to be decided without delay. He literally seized the moment.

President Habibie must be given great credit for his decisiveness. This was not a popular decision within his own government. After reports of yet another atrocity involving the murder of some East Timorese civilians, I rang President Habibie and asked to see him in Dili. He agreed. We had an hour and a half meeting. There were no advisers on either side present. It was simply him and me. He took a far greater risk in agreeing to that meeting as we conducted the conversation in English because I spoke neither Indonesian nor German. This aspect of the meeting obviously discomforted General Wiranto, the head of the Indonesian military and the Minister for Defence and Security, and his advisers. Habibie did not let his side down. He stuck very strongly to the Indonesian position.

During that meeting I asked that Australia be allowed to send some peacekeepers to the province because elements of the *Angkatan Bersenjata Republik Indonesia* (ABRI), which was re-designated the *Tentara Nasional*

Indonesia (TNI) in April 1999, seemed to be out of control. We thought they would be determined to frustrate the process. Habibie was adamant. He would not allow any peacekeepers to enter East Timor before the ballot actually took place. Habibie did not want to further alienate the military which already felt aggrieved at his decision. He did, however, agree to the insertion of more police. When an agreement was reached with the UN on a process to manage the independence ballot, additional officers from the Australian Federal Police were included in the UNAMET contingent. I felt we had secured an important concession that might better protect the local population.

Just after the ballot result was declared in early September, chaos ensued with the pro-Indonesian militias expressing their anger in a violent rampage that swept the province. It looked like it had been planned; it was certainly well organised. With news agencies sending graphic images of death and destruction from the streets of Dili and from smaller villages, more and more people began calling on the Australian Government to intervene and with force. The clamour for action escalated to the extent that I had to remind talkback radio callers and many others that the armed intervention they wanted constituted an invasion of Indonesia. East Timor was still part of the Republic of Indonesia and considered its sovereign territory. Unless and until the Australian Government was able to secure the blessing of the Indonesian Government for the dispatch of an intervention force, any military action would have amounted to an invasion and a serious violation of international law.

This explanation did not seem to trouble the advocates of force one bit. I accepted that demands for action reflected the depth of emotional feeling and the strength of political resolve in the Australian community for the East Timorese. Plainly, the Indonesian authorities had lost control of the situation in East Timor. They either would not or could not control the militias or their supporters and showed no obvious willingness to end the violence or halt the destruction of public and private property.

As I explained to the Australian people what could and could not be done, preparations were underway for the possibility that we might be invited to participate in an international intervention force. The 3rd Brigade of the Australian Army had been put on alert in the early part of 1999. If, as it finally eventuated, we were invited to contribute military personnel we would not being doing so from a standing start. At the same time, we were trying to have the Indonesian Government accept the need for an intervention to be followed by a resolution from the UN Security Council authorising the dispatch of a suitable force. Within Australia, few commentators seemed to realise the embarrassment that would be felt by Jakarta at the defacto admission that it could not manage its own internal affairs and conceded the need for international assistance. Indonesia would inevitably 'lose face' internationally in agreeing to an intervention force while its own military would be publicly humiliated in failing to contain the activities of untrained and undisciplined militias—assuming, of course, that they wanted to.

The United Nations sanctioned every stage of the operation and did not object to what was being proposed or how we intended to proceed. I recall with satisfaction my positive and productive interactions with UN Secretary-General Kofi Annan. Having in mind the very terrible events of Srebrenica during the dissolution of Yugoslavia in July 1995, the Australian Ambassador to the United States, Andrew Peacock, conveyed the strong views of Americans who had been involved, particularly Richard Holbrooke. The Dayton accords that brought an end to the tragic events of the Bosnian war were negotiated by Holbrooke. The Americans were adamant that the intervention had a sufficiently broad mandate. They wanted to ensure the fate which befell the Dutch peacekeepers in Srebrenica of being unable to stop a massacre did not befall Australian peacekeepers. We secured a very ample mandate from the Security Council which authorised an Australian-led multinational force to restore peace to the province, to protect the UNAMET contingent and to facilitate necessary humanitarian assistance. Just five days later, INTERFET was on the ground in East Timor. It would become the largest international deployment of Australian forces since the Vietnam War. In the Australian psyche, it was a very significant event and a turning point in the national mood. The Australian people were aware that this event would put the world spotlight on their country. Depending on the success or the failure of the mission, and on the conduct of Australian peacekeepers, judgements would be made about our nation and its capacity.

The deployment of INTERFET represented a remarkable diplomatic and military effort by Australia. We were immediately supported by our New

Zealand neighbours. The Prime Minister, Jenny Shipley, committed a battalion. When she, as a National prime minister (heading a centre right government), was replaced not long afterwards by Labour's Helen Clark, (heading a centre left government), one of the first things the new prime minister did was to inform me that the New Zealand commitment would remain. From the beginning, however, I did not want it to be a white Anglo-Celtic operation in the Asian region. We did receive welcome support from a detachment of Gurkha's from the British Army, a unit from the Royal Marines and 600 Canadian personnel. We soon assembled a force that drew on many nations from our neighbourhood, including significant contributions from Thailand, the Philippines and South Korea. It was not a Western intervention; it was a regional intervention.

We had some difficult moments with our American friends. I had thought the Americans would provide ground forces. During a long telephone conversation with President Bill Clinton, he indicated that putting 'American boots in the ground' was not possible. I learnt something during that conversation that I had not appreciated earlier. The Americans had extracted a substantial peace dividend from the end of the Cold War. The United States had run down its expenditure on defence so much, Clinton said very plainly, that the American military was too stretched to provide the sort of assistance we wanted. After explaining that Australia had supported the United States in a series of past wars and conflicts, I was direct in expressing my disappointment that American personnel would not be part of INTERFET. Alexander Downer decided there was merit in expressing Australia's disappointment publicly.

To his credit, Clinton got the message that we were unhappy. While he could not send troops, he provided a great deal of support with airlift, logistics, intelligence as well as diplomatic backing. There was a visit to Jakarta by the United States Secretary of Defense, William Cohen, who made it very plain that the Americans would react strongly against any attempt by the Indonesians to frustrate the progress of the intervention force. I was reminded that the United States does have a very real capacity to be able to respond to the legitimate concerns of their friends and allies. Conveniently, an APEC meeting was scheduled to be held in New Zealand at that time. It allowed me to discuss the strategic and logistical help the United States would provide directly with Clinton.

History records that INTERFET was a highly successful operation. There is a tendency to look back and think this success was inevitable. At the time, I was deeply apprehensive. Would rogue elements of the TNI and the most ardent of the militias decide to oppose the intervention? Were the Australian people ready for casualties? I recall the farewell in Townsville for the first detachment of troops heading to East Timor. We had dinner in the soldiers' mess and I remember walking back to our car and seeing a group of corporals and sergeants talking to their troops. I thought to myself: some of them may not be with us tomorrow. We could not be confident of the reception that awaited them. It is impossible to say that no-one would be hurt given the mood on the streets of Dili in particular. We could not, and did not, trust the TNI's discipline. Fortunately, the opponents of East Timorese independence were constrained when the intervention occurred thanks to the leadership of Major General Peter Cosgrove and his senior officers who managed to negotiate with their TNI counterparts an orderly entry into East Timor. Order was restored in East Timor, a transitional UN administration was established and arrangements for independent nationhood were advanced. In every respect Cosgrove brought great distinction to the leadership of INTERFET.

Twenty years on, East Timor has become a very important piece of Australian post-Cold War history. It was the first time Australia had led a major deployment abroad in its own right. In the broader socio-political context, the INTERFET commitment ended the post-Vietnam era in the Australian experience. The period between 1973 and 1999 had been seen by some observers as one of declining pride in Australia's military achievements. In the 1970s and 1980s there were even suggestions that Anzac Day would occupy a diminished place in our national life and perhaps even fade away for lack of interest. For a combination of reasons, including the legitimate pride felt by a cross-section of Australians at what was achieved by INTERFET, this did not occur.

Notwithstanding what Australia was able to do in East Timor, there were flaws in our preparedness and weaknesses in our capabilities. INTERFET revealed what we needed to do and what we needed to become as a regional military power. The present and future needs of the Australian Defence Force (ADF) would be addressed in subsequent years. The principal capability gap was transport, sometimes called 'lift', capacity. The subsequent purchase of

C-17 Galaxy transport aircraft and the *Canberra* class amphibious assault ships (LHDs) was a response to what the ADF learned in East Timor. As the subsequent Regional Assistance Mission in the Solomon Islands (RAMSI) illustrated after August 2003, an important lesson from the East Timor intervention was that Australia needed military capacity for these kinds of operations in our immediate region. The very success of Australia's intervention in East Timor meant that the world would in future look to leadership from Australia to meet the emerging challenges of our neighbourhood. In 2006, believing that Australia could face a number of situations that were similar or even more demanding than East Timor and the Solomon Islands, I announced the expansion of the Army by two extra infantry battalions.

These decisions required substantial investment from the Commonwealth and this affected the budget 'bottom line'. The magnitude of the funding required could, however, been much greater had the Coalition Government not made some firm decisions about defence outlays several years earlier. Within hours of winning office in March 1996, my government had been advised that drastic spending cuts were required to get the budget back under control. The budget contained an $8 billion deficit—it has been referred to as a 'black hole'—and net Commonwealth debt stood at $96 billion. I insisted on the exclusion of Defence from planned expenditure reductions.

Australia's improved economic (including budget) position by 1997–1998 also meant that it was not engulfed by the Asian Financial Crisis. Because the economy was strong and getting stronger, Australian was able to provide financial help to Thailand, South Korea and Indonesia at a time of dire need that included reductions in their GDP around 10 percent. There was no coincidence in Thailand and South Korea being among the largest contributors to INTERFET. I would contend that Australia's national wealth and creative leadership in this period, both financially and militarily, secured our standing and raised our profile in Asia more than the multi-lateral efforts of the preceding government. The constantly improving budget position (it was in surplus every year from 1997 to 2007), meant that Australia was able to fund INTERFET fully without resorting to a special 'East Timor levy' which had initially been foreshadowed. The East Timor invention and a number of similar events demonstrate the crucial link between economic strength and the projection of national power.

In terms of the 'machinery of government', one of the major Cabinet changes I made on becoming Prime Minister was to establish the National Security Committee (NSC) of Cabinet. This ordinarily comprised the Prime Minister, the Deputy Prime Minister, the Treasurer and, on a permanent basis, the Ministers for Defence and Foreign Affairs. The secretaries of the Departments of the Prime Minister and Cabinet, Defence and Foreign Affairs would also attend. They were joined by the heads of the Office of National Assessments (ONA) (now the Office of National Intelligence) and the Australian Security Intelligence Organisation (ASIO). Other ministers, such as the Attorney-General and the Minister for Immigration, and senior officials were invited to participate when their portfolio responsibilities were involved. Although the NSC had only met when necessary between 1996 and early 1999, it proved its worth in the prelude and execution of INTERFET. It was during a meeting of the NSC that the decision was taken that I should write what became known as the 'Habibie letter'. The NSC met frequently—sometimes daily—during the East Timor operation and proved that having a standing group of minister and officials to consider defence and security questions was a far superior arrangement to any *ad hoc* combination of experts and advisers. As the NSC became more experienced, it was able to exert greater influence.

Neither UNAMET nor INTERFET would have succeeded without the courage and competence of the men and women of the ADF and the AFP who proved to be outstanding ambassadors for this country. They were ably supported by the diplomatic and administrative talents of those serving in a number of departments, principally Defence and Foreign Affairs. As prime minister, I always felt well supplied with sound advice and insightful counsel from people who had thought long and hard about the best way to resolve an issue that had persisted for decades. That we were able to deal with the issue creatively and conscientiously is a matter of immense pride for me and this nation. Most importantly, UNAMET and INTERFET delivered liberation and freedom to the long-suffering people of East Timor. They deserved nothing less.

CHAPTER 2

A diplomatic perspective

Penny Wensley

A s Australia's Ambassador and Permanent Representative to the United Nations (UN) in New York at the time of the East Timor crisis in 1999, I was closely involved in the extensive and unprecedented diplomatic effort that secured the international intervention. Some elements of this effort are well-known, notably those conducted at a high political level, involving Prime Ministers, Presidents, Foreign Ministers and other leaders. Those activities have been the focus of considerable research and analysis and have been well-documented and recorded for history. David Connery's book *Crisis Policymaking: Australia and the ET crisis of 1999* (ANU Press, 2010) is a good example of the well-researched histories of the period.[1]

UNSC members voting unanimously in favour of resolution 1264 (1999).

Considerably less known, thought about, and discussed, however, have been the activities undertaken at the UN headquarters in New York; the diplomacy conducted there by Australia, by other countries and by the UN, that played a decisive role in delivering Security Council Resolution 1264 that authorised the mission later known as INTERFET. In part, that is because some of those activities, at the time, were conducted in secret, or deliberately kept low-key; knowledge of them held within a very small circle. In part, it is because, to my perception, other than among specialist academics, certain NGOs and areas of government departments dealing with UN agencies or handling issues on the UN agenda, there is much less interest, within Australia, in the UN and less awareness of the way it works —than in many other countries. There is a tendency for commentators in the public domain to focus on the UN's deficiencies, rather than its capabilities, and on its shortcomings rather than its successes. Additionally, in government, there is greater interest in bilateral and regional diplomacy than in multilateral diplomacy.

As a diplomat whose career spanned all three areas—bilateral postings in the Pacific, Asia, Europe, Africa and the Americas, policy work on regional organisations and issues and three multilateral postings, including seven years as Australia's Ambassador to the UN—three in Geneva and four in New York—I think that is a pity. Each of these forms of diplomacy is important and contributes to the national interest. They can be complementary and reinforcing, as we saw vividly in managing the East Timor crisis. The representations, lobbying, collection and delivery of information and intelligence, the 'advice from capitals', providing assessments and judgements about country positions or possible positions from a number of bilateral posts, fed vital information to the decision-making centres in Canberra and New York.

There are skills and capabilities—diplomatic tradecraft—common to all areas, but in a multilateral context, those of communication, representation, and negotiation—and language skills—obviously have added value and importance. In the case of the UN, recognised as a complex, challenging environment, there is an additional, specialised requirement to understand and master its complex rules, practices and procedures.

When drawing lessons from management of the East Timor crisis—of what worked, why, what delivered success—one is the importance of having well-placed Australian personnel with a good understanding of the UN, of

Ambassador Wensley addressing the UNSC 1999.

how it works and can be 'worked'. This is not something easily or quickly acquired—but rather built over years—as in my own case—through exposure to UN meetings and international negotiations. At the Australian Mission to the UN in New York in 1999, we had those capabilities and drew on them extensively. As Australia's Ambassador, I was proud of my small team and the significant contribution it made to the overall national effort.

As a general observation, today we do not have enough people with those skills and experience and there is insufficient recognition of the importance of multilateral diplomacy. There is a need to build Australian professional capability and expertise to operate effectively with the UN, to deal with an ever-expanding agenda of global challenges and threats, and to be 'operation-ready' to respond to future crises in our region and beyond. My observations encompass not only our professional diplomatic service but Australian government departments and agencies, the Australian Defence Force (ADF) and the nation's police services.

Specific lessons can very valuably be drawn from the historic Security Council resolution that authorised the intervention—and from the 'United Nations diplomacy' that enabled its adoption in the early hours of the morning of 15 September, 1999. The moment in the Security Council Chamber, when 15 hands were raised in unanimous approval of Resolution 1264, was unforgettable.[2] It was one of the highest points of my four decade career as a diplomat. It represented an enormous achievement for Australia and

Australian diplomacy; and, if not a breakthrough, then certainly a significant success for multilateral diplomacy and for the UN.

By way of background: the Security Council is the only body of the six main UN organs with the power to issue binding resolutions to member states. It has five permanent members, known as 'the P5'. They are the United Kingdom, France, the United States, China and the Russian Federation. There are also ten non-permanent members, elected on a regional basis for a two year term, by another of the UN's six main organs, the General Assembly. At the time of the East Timor crisis, Australia was not a non-permanent member. We were outside the privileged and powerful inner circle of decision-makers- making the task for Australia of securing Security Council agreement considerably more difficult. Before the actual vote, nothing was assured. It was a big 'ask' on three fronts.

First, Australia wanted Security Council authority and approval for the establishment of a multi-national force. Second, it wanted the force to be led by Australia. Third, and to use 'UN speak', Australia wanted a 'Chapter Seven mandate'. The latter relates to Chapter VII of the UN Charter which deals with 'Threats to the Peace, Breaches of the Peace and Acts of Aggression'. It spells out the measures the Security Council can authorise in order to maintain or restore international peace and security. These include measures not involving the use of armed force, for example, sanctions or the severance of diplomatic relations, or it can authorise the use of force such as military operations, which can involve the air, sea or land forces of UN member States.

Security Council mandates for the establishment of UN peace-keeping and peace-making operations that allow the use of force have varied. In the case of East Timor, Australia sought and secured what was universally considered a strong and comprhensive mandate. The force, which became known as INTERFET, was authorised 'to take all necessary measures" to fulfil its mandate.[3] This included the use of lethal weapons to protect civilians under imminent threat of physical violence. This entitlement is sometimes called the 'right to shoot'.

It is important to emphasise that the military intervention in East Timor was *not* a UN peacekeeping operation. INTERFET was a multinational non-UN peacemaking taskforce that was organised and led by Australia *in accordance with* UN Resolutions to address the humanitarian and security crisis engulfing East Timor. It operated from 20 September 1999 until the arrival of UN peacekeepers the following year as part of the UN Transitional Administration in East Timor (UNTAET).

The development of a Security Council resolution is a demanding process. In addition to requiring much formal preparatory work, it involves extensive informal diplomacy, mostly conducted behind the scenes: first, to draft and negotiate agreement on a text, then to secure sufficient support for its adoption. For the East Timor resolution, in accordance with UN Charter requirements for the adoption of a draft resolution on a non-procedural matter, we needed affirmative votes from nine of the fifteen members of the Council, including the concurring votes of the five permanent members. The final outcome, with the resolution formally presented as a consensus text of the Council and supported by all fifteen members, was deeply gratifying for everyone involved in its preparation. It was also testimony to the effectiveness of the behind-the-scenes diplomacy that preceded the vote. Much of that diplomacy was conducted by the 'Core Group'.

For a long time after the intervention, little was said or written publicly about this group or its composition. I first drew attention to its existence in February 2000 in a speech on East Timor and the UN that I delivered in Sydney to the UN Association of Australia and the Australian Institute for International Affairs.[4] On that occasion, I did not identify its members. At that time, I explained that:

> from the moment the ballot process began, Australia worked closely with a small group of other countries with a close interest in East Timor. This group, on the model of an established UN mechanism, known as Groups of Friends of the Secretary-General, was very carefully composed and kept deliberately small. It included Security Council members as well as non-members, all committed to the success of the East Timor process. The group worked in very close partnership with the UN Secretariat and operated strategically, meeting on a daily basis throughout the crisis period. Members were in constant contact 24 hours a day, sharing information, developing ideas, co-ordinating representations to others, formulating careful strategies to address

current or looming problems. The group also worked in the closest of contact with our respective capitals, all of which had established East Timor task forces or policy co-ordination groups and with our respective embassies in Jakarta.

Since those public comments in 2000, further information about the Core Group has appeared, notably in three publications. The first was a 2003 memoir written by Ambassador Jamsheed Marker, the UN Secretary General's Personal Representative for East Timor, *East Timor: A Memoir of the Negotiations for Independence.*[5] The second was a book published in 2007, by the United States Institute of Peace Press entitled *Friends Indeed? The United Nations, Groups of Friends and the Resolution of Conflict.*[6] The author, Teresa Whitfield, examined an under-studied aspect of international affairs-the use of groups of friends, contact groups, informal coalitions and core groups to support or facilitate conflict resolution. She includes a case study on the East Timor Core Group. The third was a 2016 article published in the *Australian Journal of International Affairs*, by Jeremy Farrell and Jochen Prantl, on 'Leveraging diplomatic power and influence on the Security Council: the case of Australia'.[7] Farrell and Prantl demonstrate that the Core Group's work was an instance of Australia using its diplomatic capacity, creativity and connections to exercise a high degree of influence on UN Security Council decision-making, without being on the Council.

As a member of the Core Group and someone intimately involved with its formation and operations, I can say with authority that not all the information in these publications is fully accurate—but much of it is.

The members of the Core Group were Australia, the United States, the United Kingdom, New Zealand and Japan—described later by the UN Secretariat as 'an ideal mixture of very vested and very benevolent forces'.[8] And within that group of five, it is fair to say, especially as developments reached the point of Security Council action and the drafting of Security Council resolutions, there was an inner circle of three: Australia, the United States and the United Kingdom. Each member of the group had their own idea of why they were there, of what needed to be done, and how they could contribute to its work.

The UN Secretariat, which is sometimes called 'The sixth Permanent Member of the Security Council', and with good reason, had its own very definite and clear views on the 'who and why' of membership as shared with Teresa Whitfield by senior secretariat officials. Drawing on their comments, she remarked:

> the composition of the Core Group was carefully balanced. It responded to a variety of needs, all of which would be facilitated by its small size. These included the coordination of international efforts behind a United Nations lead; information sharing as the political process advanced, political leverage, particularly over Indonesia; and logistical and financial support through a Trust Fund established for this purpose.[9]

Australia's inclusion, and my own inclusion, was certain. I was in regular, close contact with the Secretary General, Kofi Annan and his Chief of Staff, Iqbal Riza, and with Ambassador Marker. I had their confidence. I had built good relationships with all the Ambassadors whose governments had an interest in East Timor, including the Portuguese Ambassador, with whom I had also been holding regular meetings. I had established equally good lines of communication and access to relevant, key areas of the UN Secretariat, notably the Departments of Political Affairs (DPA) and Peace-Keeping Operations (DPKO). The Australian Mission was also working extremely closely with the Secretariat—although its agenda in setting up the Core Group was somewhat different from our own. Was it a coincidence that the idea took hold just at the same time Australia was talking about forming a larger support group? I think not.

The choice of members was highly strategic. Again citing UN Secretariat sources Whitfield observed:

> A group without Australia was clearly inconceivable: its close links with Indonesia, long history on East Timor, geographic position and ample resources to support a UN operation placed it in a unique position, Moreover it had much at stake in a positive outcome. The Secretariat was in regular contact with Australia's permanent representative, Ambassador Penny Wensley. Although officials would come to see Australia playing a 'Jekyll and Hyde' role with respect to its relations with Indonesia… they knew that Australia's close cooperation would be essential to any success. Australia's leading role on the issue was

one readily recognised by the other states involved and was reflected in the tendency for Australia to speak first in most Core Group meetings. The US was also an inevitable choice.[10]

Whitfield further observed:

Japan was an important, (though usually fairly silent) member of the group. It was the largest donor to Indonesia and despite economic troubles of its own, had been deeply involved in efforts to help Indonesia through its financial crisis … Although Japan's constitution included strict provisions preventing its military from participating in PKO's (peace-keeping operations), Japan was eager for enhanced engagement with the UN in peace and security and promised substantial financial support for any UN operations in East Timor.

The Secretariat counted on Japan's presence to offer reassurance to Indonesia and its supporters on the Security Council and to bring some balance to an otherwise overwhelming anglophone membership. The inclusion of New Zealand and the United Kingdom was also a matter of strategic utility. "New Zealand brought regional expertise, coupled with deep sympathy for the Timorese cause, that the Secretariat believed could provide a useful foil to its larger and more powerful neighbour, Australia". As for the UK, it was considered "a somewhat surprising choice". They had no obvious interest in the East Timor issue and hadn't sought an active role. But the Secretariat thought that the UK would be well placed to pilot consideration of the Resolution through the Security Council—not least because its remove would give it greater impartiality.[11]

And they were spot-on in that judgement. From my perspective, the United Kingdom Mission's experience, as a Permanent Member of the Security Council, was invaluable. It was enormously helpful when we moved into drafting Presidential statements and Security Council resolutions. In addition, the British took their Core Group responsibilities elsewhere with their Ambassador to Indonesia coordinating useful parallel meetings of the group in Jakarta.

Once established, the Group worked extremely well. Initially, we met without UN Secretariat officials present, but as the tempo quickened, we moved to having a Secretariat presence. The Group was active over many months and operated at several levels, drawing on professional resources in our respective missions. Small drafting committees were set up to focus on and work through particular issues. And throughout the process, through those many months, working closely with the Secretary-General and his senior colleagues and advisers, we maintained the strictest confidence.

This strict approach sometimes annoyed other colleagues, good friends included. The Canadian Ambassador was an example. When I refused to discuss the draft Security Council Resolution with him, on 14 September, 1999, he sent me a stinging hand-written note about not honouring the spirit of CANZ cooperation. That hurt. The co-operation between Canada, Australia and New Zealand in multilateral forums is a long-established and very important aspect of the diplomatic practice of all three countries. But I had to maintain the confidentiality of the Core Group's work. The stakes were too high and things were so uncertain. This remained true to the time of the vote. While critical elements were still being discussed and explored, we could not afford to share information beyond the inner circle, knowing that there were elements hostile to our purpose.

The quiet, intensive diplomacy conducted by the Core Group over a sustained period, was a fundamental element of the 'UN diplomacy' on East Timor that delivered Security Council agreement for the intervention. In his Memoir, Ambassador Marker describes it as becoming an 'essential part of the negotiating process'.[12] Marker's recollections underline the length of time the group operated, that is, many months before developments in East Timor reached crisis point. They also make clear that the 'formal' Core Group, as described by Whitfield and her UN Secretariat contacts, had more informal origins, emerging from the activities and initiatives of a small group of professional diplomats, whose governments had strong interest in the East Timor issue. Marker commented:

> In addition, we were fortunate enough to have the invaluable help, advice and support of a number of very able diplomats posted to missions to the UN. Most prominent of these were Ambassador Penny Wensley of

Australia, US Alternative Representative, Ambassador Nancy Soderberg, UK Deputy Head of Mission, Ambassador Stewart Eldon, Ambassador Yukio Takasu of Japan and New Zealand Ambassador Michael Powles.

They met me shortly after I took over the assignment (early 1999) and conveyed to me their interest and support for the East Timor negotiations. They were true to their offer in word and deed, providing me with important information and intelligence obtained from their governments-the value of which was immeasurably bolstered by the supplementary advice rendered through the personal skills of the diplomats themselves. Later on, these representatives were to form the Core Group of unofficial advisers on East Timor.

The role played by the Core Group offers clear lessons on the timing and circumstances in which an informal group of states may helpfully be enlisted to increase the efficacy of UN action.[13]

I have focused in this chapter on the Core Group because it is a story not known to many people. I also think it offers some important insights into aspects of ' UN diplomacy', including the way the Secretariat works, and the Secretary General himself worked. Quiet diplomacy was his forte. Kofi Annan's hand was everywhere. He was a consummate diplomat and leader, who, from the time he assumed the office of Secretary General in January 1997, as Ambassador Marker put it in his memoir, had 'signalled his personal and active commitment to a solution of the East Timor problem'.[14] And as the events of 1999 played out, he intensified that commitment.

Although this volume focuses on the events of 1999, it is worth recalling that East Timor had been a regular item on the UN agenda for more than two decades, since 1975. In November 1976, the General Assembly rejected the Indonesian Government's legislation incorporating East Timor as a province of Indonesia and called for an act of self-determination. Subsequent General Assembly and Security Council resolutions initiated a process which required negotiations between Indonesia and Portugal, under the aegis of the Secretary General, to resolve the question of East Timor. These proceeded in a desultory, lack-lustre fashion until Kofi Annan became Secretary-General and decided that the East Timor issue needed a push and a more vigorous approach. One of his first acts as Secretary General was to create a new position—the Secretary General's Personal Representative for East Timor—and to appoint

Ambassador Jamsheed Marker to the role. Ambassador Marker would report directly to the Secretary-General and as required, to the Security Council.

The East Timor intervention is widely acclaimed as a success and success, always, has many parents. But I can say from first-hand involvement that the Secretary-General played a critical role. The chapter on the East Timor Intervention in his own memoir, published in 2012, *Interventions: a life in War and Peace*,[15] is both compelling reading and eloquent testimony to his deep personal engagement and contribution to the international community's response to the East Timor crisis. In his Memoir, Ambassador Marker also paid strong tribute to the Secretary-General:

> Kofi Annan's role in the East Timor negotiations was absolutely crucial and its importance cannot be emphasised enough. It went far beyond the titular and involved an active, lively interest in the progress of the process, spurred when necessary by effective initiatives and interventions … Despite the multifarious other issues that landed on the desk of the Secretary-General, Kofi always possessed an up-to-date knowledge of the current state of negotiations over East Timor.[16]

The Secretary-General's leadership and decisiveness at critical moments was outstanding. However, there were others, too, who took bold and decisive action to move things in the right direction, towards that final vote in the Security Council and those fifteen hands raised in approval of the binding resolution authorising the intervention.

Two such actions stand out. The first was the resurrection, at the suggestion of the Secretariat, of a device which had not been used for many years by the Council: the sending of a small mission of Security Council members to see for themselves what was happening on the ground and assess the situation at first-hand. The second was the holding of a Security Council Open Debate on East Timor. The Mission, five members of the Security Council and a senior Secretariat official, visited Dili and Jakarta between 8–12 September. The Open Debate was held on 11 September 1999.

I have paid public tribute before, and do so again—to the courage and determination of the then President of the Security Council—Netherlands Ambassador Peter Van Walsum, for insisting, against considerable resistance, on going ahead, on a Saturday, with what turned into a seven hour debate in which 51 countries participated, including of course, Australia. That debate sent an unmistakeable message to Indonesia. The fact that the Indonesian government accepted the offer of a multinational security force the next day, on 12 September, was proof positive of its worth and impact. Similarly, the Council Mission had a big impact, galvanising the Council into action. Several members of the Mission were deeply affected by the evidence of the wholesale destruction and their personal observations clearly influenced the views of other Council members previously reluctant to support a robust Resolution. From our perspective, when that Mission returned to New York from Dili and Jakarta, its report to the Security Council on 14 September, 1999 overcame any lingering resistance in the Council to the passage of a strong resolution mandating the multinational force.

Van Walsum identified other factors behind adoption of Resolution 1264 (the "INTERFET" Resolution).[17] In his view, 'what had done the trick', leading Indonesia to accept the offer of a multinational security force, was President Clinton's announcement on 11 September 1999 that all American military assistance programs to Indonesia would be suspended.[18] His analysis underlines the many factors and forces at work, in Jakarta, Canberra, Washington and elsewhere,to address the East Timor crisis. All this effort, in different ways, contributed to the outcome achieved in the Security Council: unanimous approval of a strong resolution authorising the intervention.

For readers unfamiliar with the UN and the world of multilateral diplomacy, it may be difficult to appreciate the challenges associated with getting fifteen members of the Security Council to agree on a tough course of action. I hope in this chapter, I have given some glimpse of its workings and possibilities and a sharpened understanding of the way the UN and member states can work together to achieve results. The East Timor crisis enabled us to test, in a practical way, many ways of working and their effectiveness. Some of those things—quiet diplomacy, the formation of a Core Group, the use of an investigative mission and the holding of an open debate in the Security Council - proved their worth and could readily be replicated in other situations.

Part of the legacy of the East Timor intervention should be greater acknowledgement of the role that professional diplomacy played, in the UN context, in securing the intervention and of the benefits that close Australia-UN cooperation can deliver when important national interests are at stake. Credit where credit is due. The UN has its flaws and shortcomings, but we should not underestimate its capabilities. A key lesson learned from 1999 was the value of having Australians who know how to work with, and within the UN. Capacity in multilateral diplomacy is a valuable national asset which we should not underrate or diminish. Instead it should be strengthened and celebrated.

Minister Downer addressing the UNSC 1999, Ambassador Wensley behind.

Endnotes

1   David Connery, *Crisis Policymaking: Australia and the East Timor Crisis of 1999*, ANU Press, 2010.

2   UNSC Resolution 1264, 'The Situation in East Timor', UN Doc. S/RES/1264 (15 September 1999) (adopted unanimously).

3   UNSC Res 1264, operative para 3.

4   Penny Wensley, 'East Timor and the United Nations', Speech to the Australian Institute for International Affairs, New South Wales Branch, Sydney, 23 February 2000.

5   Jamsheed Marker, *East Timor: A Memoir of the Negotiations for Independence*, Macfarlane and Co., 2003.

6   Teresa Whitfield, *Friends Indeed? The United Nations, Groups of Friends and the Resolution of Conflict*, United States Institute of Peace Press, 2007.

7   Jeremy Farrell and Jochen Prantl, 'Leveraging Diplomatic Power and Influence on the Security Council: the Case of Australia', *Australian Journal of International Affairs*, vol. 70, no. 6, 2016, pp. 601-612.

8   UN official, interviewed on 2 March 2004, cited in Whitfield, p. 201.

9   Whitfield, *Friends Indeed?*, p. 201.

10 Whitfield, referring to Wensley, *Friends Indeed?*, p. 201.

11 Whitfield, *Friends Indeed?*, p. 202.

12 Marker, *East Timor: A Memoir*, p. 15.

13 Marker, *East Timor: A Memoir*, pp. 14–15.

14 Marker, East Timor: A Memoir, p. 10

15 Kofi Annan with Nader Mousavizadeh, 'Sovereignty and Human Rights: Kosovo, East Timor, Darfur, and the Responsibility to Protect', chapter 3 in *Interventions: A Life in War and Peace*, Penguin Press, 2012, pp. 81-133.

16 Marker, *East Timor: A Memoir*, pp. 11-12.

17 Peter Van Walsum, 'Peter Van Walsum Talks about the Interventions of 1999: Kosovo and East Timor', edited text of a speech delivered on 18 February 2014 in The Hague, on the Dutch Presidency of the UN Security Council in September 1999 (9 August 2014), <http://nvvn.nl/peter-van-walsum-talks-about-the-interventions-of-1999-kosovo-and-east-timor/>.

18 Van Walsum, 'Peter Van Walsum Talks about the Interventions of 1999'.

CHAPTER 3

An industry perspective

Michael Ward

The deployment of an Australian-led international intervention force in East Timor in 1999 marked an important turning point in the nation's life. It was also an important time for me. My last role as a full-time Australian Army officer before joining industry was a secondment to serve as Secretary of the Joint Standing Committee on Foreign Affairs, Defence and Trade. One of my final tasks was accompanying committee members to East Timor once the situation had stabilised after the militia rampage. I recall how impressed we were with both the Australian mission's achievements and the extent to which Australia's own interests had been advanced. My contribution to this volume is considering the legacy of East Timor on commercial and business support for ADF operations and to chart the major shifts that have occurred in defence industry since 1999.

Industry was not regarded a key component of national defence capability in 1999. On one side there was the government-owned Australian Defence Industries (ADI) which had been corporatised a decade earlier. It brought together the remaining defence industry facilities still operated by the Commonwealth, such as the Garden Island naval dockyard, the Lithgow Small Arms Factory and munitions manufacturers in Victoria. The Government wanted ADI to be more financially sustainable and moved towards its eventual privatisation although observers noted it took many years to change the culture of what was then a highly bureaucratised and inefficient organisation. The Australian Submarine Corporation, then owned by a joint venture led by the Swedish defence supplier Kockums, and the Commonwealth, was responsible for building the *Collins* class submarines and had encountered a number of technical difficulties and organisational problems. Bucking the trend towards privatisation, the business was actually brought into full government ownership in 2000.

There were numerous other private companies, many with international parents, that had maintained a long-term presence in Australia. They were beginning to see the potential of an Australian defence industry and benefitting from increases in outsourcing a range of defence support functions. There was still, however, an under-investment in the Australian market by the large defence multinationals. To a significant degree, many defence companies were little more than shopfronts for the sale of foreign produced military equipment. With a few exceptions, industry was the arms-length provider of goods and services.

The Howard Government had been aware for some time that Australian defence industry had unfulfilled potential and closer collaboration made sense. The release of *Defence and industry: Strategic Policy Statement* in June 1998 heralded the Coalition's determination to nurture a locally-sustainable and internationally-competitive defence industry. The Government's focus was to ensure 'a sustainable and competitive defence industry base, able to support a technologically-advanced ADF' and called for 'efficient, innovative and durable industries—and a close partnership between Defence and those industries'.

For overseas-based companies it was apparent that a condition of gaining access to Defence work would be a demonstration of a long term commitment to Australia. Within a relatively short time, many of those multi-nationals, Raytheon included, responded by establishing full subsidiaries in Australia. Significant investments in people, plant and equipment, tools and processes accompanied these commitments. These investments were only possible as a consequence of the Defence White Paper of December 2000 which itself was greatly influenced by the capability lessons Australia had learned from the intervention in East Timor.

Australia's maritime capability illustrates this point vividly. Of the 22 nations that participated in the international intervention force (INTERFET),

10 provided naval assets. Australia may have been the largest contributor of vessels but countries such as the United States, the United Kingdom, France, Singapore, New Zealand, Canada and others all deployed ships. In 2000, the then Director of Navy's Sea Power Centre, Captain (later, Rear Admiral) James Goldrick, noted the importance of maritime forces creating a protective umbrella within which the land component could operate. In East Timor, force protection was provided by the US Navy's Aegis cruiser, USS *Mobile Bay*, and the Royal Navy destroyer, HMS *Glasgow*, as well.

As Goldrick observed, the deployment of capable surface combatants was a clear signal of INTERFET's resolve and its capacity for self-defence. HMS *Glasgow*, operating with Australia's FFG-7 class frigates, also provided air warfare surveillance and combat capability. But Goldrick singled out the American Aegis cruiser as a vital enabler in the operation's opening stages:

> Her long range air-warfare systems, both in sensors and weaponry and her excellent battle management and command capability meant that the force could contemplate any situation with a high degree of confidence, even without the continuous presence of friendly fighter aircraft.

The INTERFET Commander, Major General (later General) Peter Cosgrove made a similar observation in an address delivered at Georgetown University in 2000 when speaking of the utility of sea power. He explained: 'the persuasive, intimidatory or deterrent nature of major warships was not to me as the combined joint force commander an incidental, nice to have "add-on" but an important indicator of national and international resolve'. The civilian defence analyst, Alan Ryan, also pointed to the continuing presence of two American amphibious assault ships with a contingent of marines and heavy lift helicopters as providing a significant show of force, a key affirmation of American support and essential to expanding INTEFET's authority.

In relation to Australia's deployed forces, Goldrick noted the absence of an afloat headquarters while the existing three ship sealift capability proved to be inadequate. There was, according to David Stevens of the Sea Power Centre,

> [a] most significant shortfall ... in heavy sealift, due in part to delays in modernising two *Newport* class amphibious transports purchased from the

US Navy in 1994 [HMA Ships *Kanimbla* and *Manoora*]. This left available only the heavy lift ship HMAS *Tobruk*, which was itself long overdue for an extended maintenance period.

There was a notional capability but, in practice, it was inadequate. The shortfall was remedied by chartering a civilian fast wave-piercing catamaran, HMAS *Jervis Bay*, which transported troops and supplies. It was a timely measure that filled a key capability gap. This was more a case of good luck than good management.

The 2000 Defence White Paper, of which nine pages were devoted to defence industry, was drafted with the INTERFET experience very much in mind. It commented on the success of East Timor and observed that: 'INTERFET also provided an invaluable opportunity to test and evaluate many aspects of our military capabilities, and to learn how we could do things better. The Government has drawn on these lessons in this White Paper'. The document made specific reference to the lessons of INTERFET in the context of deploying forces and supporting them once deployed. This reflection included the amphibious lift capability and the need for eventual replacement of *Manoora* and *Kanimbla*—which were always intended to be short-term options. The Government eventually decided to acquire two Landing Helicopter Dock (LHD) ships, *Adelaide* and *Canberra*.

Significantly, the White Paper also identified the need for at least three air-defence capable ships that would be much larger and more capable that the guided missile frigates they would replace. The Air Warfare Destroyers (AWDs) with their Aegis weapons system was the result. These acquisitions and others outlined in the White Paper have not only transformed Australia's military capability but they have prompted, if not necessitated, a transformation in defence industry as a whole. This particular White Paper afforded industry an important opportunity to generate new skills and capabilities, including essential systems engineering and integration skills across a range of platforms, production skills in the construction of new ships and land vehicles, the development of airborne early warning and control aircraft systems, and a range of communications, command and control and information systems.

In Raytheon's case, for example, the need to replace the combat system in the *Collins* class submarines allowed the company to build a systems integration capability that has been the envy of the industry. Our specialist workforce was able to provide the core capability, a capability that we later utilised as a combat system integrator for the Air Warfare Destroyer, to achieve the incredibly complex integration of the Aegis weapon system with other combat system elements. With hindsight, what Raytheon began to see two decades ago was an awakening. While there will always be a requirement for Defence to purchase equipment and services, modern warfighting capabilities would require something far more sophisticated. The most pressing need was for enterprise architectures that were populated not by products but by interoperable, integrated systems. Equally, supporting those capabilities would require more than the delivery of individual logistical solutions but the provision of sophisticated integrated logistic systems.

What especially encouraged industry investment in the 2000 White Paper was a new approach to capability planning through a detailed, bi-partisan, costed and publicly declared commitment to a ten-year Defence Capability Plan (DCP) that was to be regularly revised in response to changing strategic circumstances. It is fair to say that industry took successive copies of the DCP 'to the bank' or, more literally, to their multi-national parents, to attract foreign investment to the Australian market. This document not only outlined a catalogue of capabilities Defence was seeking to acquire, it was a fair indication of how much the Commonwealth was willing to spend in addition to providing a timeline for precisely when those procurements were to be made. Starting with the 1998 defence industry statement, continuing with the White Paper and culminating in the DCP, these documents set a high water mark for political transparency and public commitment.

Throughout the remaining years of the Howard Government and on the back of considerable private sector investment, there developed a maturity both in the capabilities of industry and the nature of the relationship between government, defence and industry. The relationship evolved into a genuine partnership as contracting became more performance based with rewards for businesses ready to accept risk. Over the next five years the industry experienced a period of consolidation. A consequence of ownership changes in large defence companies overseas, it was also due to local mergers and acquisitions including the transfer of ADI to Thales in 2006 and the acquisition of the privately-owned Australian company, Tenix Defence, by BAE Systems in 2008.

Ten years after the 2000 Defence White Paper was released, Australia was spending slightly under 2 per cent of GDP on defence. Industry could boast a workforce of 29,000 people and turnover running into billions of dollars. Abruptly, things then changed. The 2009 Defence White Paper, the first produced by a Labor Government in 20 years, was a cogent document in itself. The problem was the absence of secure and stable funding to support its aspirations and ambitions. With the Global Financial Crisis and budget deficits, defence outlays were reduced and investment was deferred. Former senior Defence official, Ross Babbage, observed:

> When the Labor government was elected in 2007 it did so on a platform of maintaining the Coalition's long-running trajectory of 3 per cent real growth in defence spending a year. Then in the 2009 Defence White Paper the government committed itself to 3 per cent real growth to 2017–18 and 2.2 per cent real growth from then until 2030. However, the reality is that since the government was elected it has delivered 3 per cent real growth in only three of the six defence budgets it has brought down. What is worse is that in 2010–11 it cut the defence budget by almost 5 per cent and then in the recent budget it cut defence spending again by 10.47 per cent. This reduces Australian defence spending to 1.56 per cent of GDP, *the lowest it has been since 1938.* By contrast the US is spending 4.7 per cent of GDP on defence, Britain 2.6 per cent, South Korea 2.5 per cent and Singapore 3.6 per cent [emphasis added].

The shortfall was not addressed until 2013.

The Coalition's election pledge to return defence spending to 2 per cent of GDP followed by an equally firm and far-sighted Defence White Paper in 2016 restored confidence within the industry. It further boosted business confidence. The 2014–2015 First Principles Review heralded much needed change to the defence organisation including introducing a 'smart buyer' model for procurement that could obviate protracted defence acquisitions in certain circumstances.

My main observation of the foremost long-term legacy of the 1999 East Timor intervention is in the contents of the 2016 White Paper. Local builds for both the future submarine and future frigate could not, and would not, have been possible without the industry capability built up in the new combat system for *Collins* class submarines as well as the complex AWD and LHD programmes in the wake of the INTERFET experience. Nor would these new projects have been possible but for the maturing relationship between defence and industry that has developed since the 2000 White Paper.

We often look at the legacy of Australia's leadership of INTERFET in terms of liberating an oppressed people, helping to create a proud new nation, exercising formidable diplomatic and military skill to forge an effective coalition of like-minded nations in the space of a few weeks. But in committing to an array of capability projects after the East Timor intervention, Australia also built a defence industry that is now a fundamental and enduring input to the nation's capability. Defence has become a seasoned, sophisticated and skilled industry that is ready and willing to take on new challenges. Widened participation of the private sector in Australia's defence and security deeply now undergirds the peace and prosperity the nation enjoys.

CHAPTER 4

UNAMET: a military perspective[1]

Paul Symon

Largely unsung, the unarmed UNAMET behaved with exemplary courage under constant harassment from militia in both the lead-up to the ballot and the days which followed.[2]

John McCarthy

The passage of time has a remarkable influence on memory. The past is never fixed. Although the events we bring to mind cannot be altered, what we make of them is never static. We draw different things from what we experience and attach new meanings or deeper significance to people and places as we reflect from the vantage point of elapsed time. Two decades ago I was sent to East Timor on a mission that had profound personal and professional impact. This chapter contains my reflections on what happened, what I learned, and what I believe the Army gained from this tumultuous period in regional affairs.[3]

The Australian Defence Force (ADF) contingent that I led during 1999 was small in comparison to the Australian Federal Police (AFP) component of what became known as UNAMET: the United Nations Mission in East Timor. Our job was 'to organise and conduct a popular consultation to ascertain whether the East Timorese people accepted a special autonomy within Indonesia or rejected the proposed special autonomy, leading to East

Timor's separation from Indonesia.'[4] Those who participated in this mission shared some deeply troubling experiences and we still reflect on our small but important role in delivering a ballot on self-determination to the courageous people of East Timor. The accompanying illustrations provide some insight into these experiences and the conditions under which were operating.

Perhaps unexpectedly for some readers, I wish to pay tribute to the small band of journalists, predominantly Australian, whose personal courage and professional dedication we observed firsthand. It was principally the journalists who brought news of this unfolding crisis to the world, especially in the days and weeks following the announcement of the ballot's outcome. The Australian public were outraged by the sounds and sights reported by the journalists who faced hardship and danger in simply doing their job.

I had little warning that I was to play a part in the long struggle of the East Timorese people for freedom. I had known of the troubles in East Timor before I joined the Royal Military College, Duntroon, in January 1979. But regimental life through the 80's and 90's distracted me from world affairs while I sought to master technical artillery and leadership skills more broadly. Now 20 years into my military career, I was having a particularly busy but rewarding time commanding an Army unit in Brisbane. Due of a large influx of new recruits through the 'Ready Reserve Scheme', I had been placed in charge of running a recruit course in addition to fulfilling my unit command responsibilities. I had no choice but to work through Christmas. We had just celebrated our unit's 50th anniversary when Major General Peter Cosgrove, the Commander of the 1st Division, contacted me by phone and said:

> Paul, interesting developments in East Timor. You're flying to Canberra tomorrow to get briefings from the intelligence agencies. You're then flying to Sydney on Wednesday to go to HQ Australian Theatre for operational briefings. On Thursday front up to your unit and say goodbye. On Friday, say goodbye to your family; you're on a plane to New York because you're writing the United Nations concept of operations (CONOPS) for a military observer component in East Timor. Are there any questions?

My mind was racing with a funny and clever response like: 'Any [expletive] questions?' I had dozens of questions ranging from 'why me?' to 'do I have a choice'. I knew from experience that when you worked for General Cosgrove in those days it was more apt simply to respond with: 'No, Sir. That is all perfectly clear.'

The first six months of 1999 were a whirlwind of activity. On 11 June, and after much deliberation, the UN passed Resolution 1246. It comprised several components. The main task was to organise and conduct a popular consultation on the basis of a direct, secret and universal ballot. The political component involved monitoring the fairness of the campaigning environment. There was also an electoral component; an information component to explain the 5 May General Agreement between the governments of Indonesia and Portugal;[5] a civilian police component of up to 280 officers to act as advisers to the Indonesian police in discharging their duties; and a military liaison component of up to 50 personnel.

The main tasks of our military component were to liaise with the *Tentara Nasional Indonesia* (TNI—the Indonesian military) and the security arm of the National Congress for Timorese Reconstruction (CNRT—the military arm of the local independence movement Falantil). In offering perspectives and providing advice to the UN Special Representative of the Secretary-General (SRSG), Ian Martin, we had to deal with the Indonesian military, Falantil and the local pro-Indonesian militia leaders. We invested a great deal of time and effort developing these three extraordinarily diverse and divergent partnerships. Just prior to deploying, I had started to read a book by former Chief of the United States Army, General Gordon Sullivan, entitled *Hope is not a Method*. I later took the book with me to East Timor. I confess that for me and my contingent, and I know for the AFP members of the mission as well, there were many days where we knew what we needed to do but did feel that 'hope was not a method'. We were gripped with a palpable sense that all of this could go terribly wrong.

As we settled into a routine we gained a better sense of how the UN would operate. As an organization the UN can move quickly when it must. When a fleet of UN vehicles rolled out of a huge Russian Antonov transport aircraft at Baucau within a few weeks of our arrival, we were impressed. These vehicles were funded by the Japanese and surplus to demand at the time. It soon became apparent that UN member countries can contribute in many positive ways if the political climate is right. Japan wanted to be seen as a

Figure 1:   My office as the UNAMET Chief of Operations at the end of week one.

Figure 2:   Major John Gould observing the arrival of UN vehicles from Japan at Bacau.

good international citizen and its logistical support to a small mission like ours was extraordinarily important.

lan Martin was in overall charge of the mission and carried heavy responsibilities. He came from an international aid background and brought a decidedly humanitarian emphasis to UNAMET's work. A man of great heart, Ian recognised that understanding the security situation from a military perspective was an area in which he needed expertise and trusted advisers. He made full use of what we had to offer and generously encouraged my team.

Figure 3:　　　　UN Special Representative Ian Martin

Figure 4:　　　Special Representative Ian Martin and senior AFP officer Alan Mills

The senior Australian police officer was Alan Mills. He, too, possessed a very steady hand. He led a large police contingent and had a direct line of communication with the Prime Minister, John Howard, which was crucial during in the mission's more difficult days. There was close rapport between the military and policy contingents as we had shared responsibilities in dealing with common security related issues.

Similarly, the importance of military relationships to the success of the mission should not be under-estimated. TNI Colonel Tono Suratman was Commander of Korem 164. As the ballot drew nearer, he was moved out of the country and replaced by Colonel Noer Muis. Coincidentally, six years before the mission I had been a classmate of Muis at the Australian Command and

Staff College in Canberra. Having a prior personal friendship with him made a difference. Following declaration of the ballot result, when law and order had completely broken down, and international staff were unable to leave the UN compound, I was given permission to move into his headquarters to broker arrangements with the TNI.

Figure 5:   The other side of the negotiating table

As part of our mandate, we interacted closely with the pro-independence movement. They were a highly disciplined community having endured more than two decades of insurgent warfare against the far superior TNI forces deployed to East Timor. Falintil was plainly one of the great human intelligence organisations of its time. It enjoyed the confidence and could rely on the support of the local people through the province. Falintil had also penetrated the pro-Indonesian militias and the TNI. The full story of their inside knowledge has never been documented but my assumption was, and remains, that both the militias and the TNI were seriously compromised. In observing and reporting on the security environment, which was both complex and controversial, we also met with militia leaders such as Jose Tavares and Eurico Guterres. We naturally strived to remain objective and neutral but we could not help but compare and contrast the type of individuals who were leading the pro-Indonesian militias with people like Taur Matan Ruak, the Falantil leader. The difference was stark. Both Tavares and Guterres were later sought by UN War Crimes prosecutors.

Figure 6:   John Gould and (the future) Prime Minister and President of East Timor, Taur Matan Ruak (TMR)

Figure 7:   The Falintil cantonment in Waimori

In the course of three months we witnessed many incidents that challenged our mandate and affronted our conscience. Very early in the deployment there was an occasion when internally displaced persons (IDP) were moving from an IDP camp through Liquica. One convoy, which the UN was seeking to escort and protect, was stopped by militias. They were armed with machetes and seemed very willing to use them. The IDPs were afraid and panicked. My team, none of whom were armed, had to deal with extraordinary circumstances such as these on an all too regular basis. In these situations we could only presume on the personal courage and the professional judgement of those officers who had been hobbled together at such short notice. Little had prepared them for these challenges. They relied on their values and the virtues that had been inculcated during their military careers—and their innate sense of decency as human beings. We all found ourselves reflecting on difficult and demanding situations in which it felt like 'hope was simply not going to be a sound method'. Twenty years on, I continue to wonder why so many more tragedies were averted or avoided. The experience of that convoy in Liquica, and similar incidents on many other days, made us ever conscious that we were treading on tenuous ground. Calamity was never far away and there was no room for complacency in managing desperate people in dangerous situations.

It eventually became apparent that there were two different chains of command operating in the province. We were trying to help the UN generally and the SRSG, Ian Martin, particularly understand that with the TNI and the militias there was a chain of command that flowed to the highest levels of the Indonesian uniformed hierarchy. We also observed that a significant number of other intelligence officials or retired intelligence generals, who were either in East Timor or elsewhere, were part of a 'shadow' chain of command working in parallel to the military chain of command. We never quite got to the bottom of this diarchal arrangement and we were not privy to all the available intelligence. But it was clear to me that Jakarta was fully aware of what was happening in its distant 27th province.

In trying to understand the security situation and anticipate looming challenges to our mandate, we were pro-active and transparent in our dealings with the militia leaders and the Falintil leaders. Inevitably, given all that was at stake, there was a great deal of suspicion about our motives and what exactly we were doing. Was the UN siding with or against the Indonesian Government? Were our conversations with the Falintil leaders giving them and their activities a political and legal legitimacy to which they were not entitled? We felt increasingly exposed to pressure from both sides as we 'fought for information'. As the ballot date came nearer, we were delivered death threats. They were probably to be expected given the enormous significance of the ballot and the dire consequences for the losing side. We were determined to preserve our discipline while watching out for each other's safety and security. But we would not be intimidated or distracted from our task.

One of the Indonesian intelligence generals in Dili made it known that Australian military liaison officers should stop being aggressive in their dealings with the pro-integration factions. There were many other warnings of this kind from those who wanted East Timor to remain within the Republic of Indonesia. They presumed the majority of East Timorese were not in favour of independence because they thought the practical benefits of being part of Indonesia exceeded the appeal of political freedom. We endeavoured to be even-handed so that, at the very least, we did not make things worse. Therein lay the challenge. Accusations of bias were easy to make and difficult to refute. We were also constrained from drawing attention to the weakness of the Indonesian National Police (POLRI) which had been given primacy in dealing with the internal security situation. POLRI was separated from the TNI on 1 April 1999, little more than two months before we deployed to East Timor. It was very clear to senior POLRI officers that while they were ostensibly running security in East Timor, they remained subordinate to the historical power and authority of the TNI commanders.

On 30 August 1999, the East Timorese were asked to answer two questions:

Do you *accept* the proposed special autonomy for East Timor within the Unitary State of the Republic of Indonesia?

Do you *reject* the proposed special autonomy for East Timor, leading to East Timor's separation from Indonesia?

The result was overwhelming in favour of independence: 78.5 percent of the population opted for separation from Indonesia. Once the results were announced by the UN Secretary-General on 4 September, local evacuations took place over the following week across 13 regions. It felt like we were following a tightly formulated script as events played out according to a pattern in each location. In each of the regions UN personnel would find themselves under attack as live rounds would be fired into their compound. The UN would then be advised that the safety of UN personnel could no longer be guaranteed. This advice would lead to emergency planning. Undeterred, the UN workers toiled day and night to remain in place. With very few resources my team evacuated almost everyone from these regional locations without harm, notwithstanding the menacing warning that their safety could not be guaranteed.

I had suspected for some time that the whole exercise might play out in this way. The intelligence I had received prior to deploying was good. It was high quality; accurate and reliable. Preventing what might have seemed inevitable was another matter. We were constrained in what we could do from the day we arrived—practically and politically. The hard part for the military component was the limited resources that were at our disposal to deal with the number of people we needed to recover safely and securely. We had to work out how best to sequence and organise the task. We could not be sure where and when the greatest challenges to the process and the most serious threats to UN personnel would be exerted. The conduct of those seeking to frustrate the whole process could not be predicted. We had to be tremendously flexible.

During the descent into chaos that followed the ballot declaration, I co-located myself with Colonel Muis in his headquarters. We had many fruitful, and also unfruitful, discussions about what was happening on the ground and why it had occurred. The UN, of course, lost its 'eyes and ears' as soon as the evacuations folded into the major population centres of Dili and Baucau. I tried to understand what was happening beyond the UN compounds while trying to exploit my relationship with Muis in order to moderate the worst excesses of the rampage rapidly engulfing the province. Figures 8 and 9 convey the senseless violence that erupted by those who decided to deny East Timor the vital infrastructure it needed following its separation from Indonesia. I was convinced that the mindless rampage was carefully planned. A great deal of effort was needed to cause so much damage. It not happen without forethought.

Figure 8:　　　　　　　　　A burnt out building in Dili

Figure 9:　　　　　　　A destroyed compound in Dili

Figure 10:   My burnt and ransacked room at the Turismo Hotel

Figure 11:   Trying to call home from Dili.

In addition to achieving the overall objectives of the mission, I was also responsible for the well-being of those under my national command. For 'social welfare' purposes, the Army had provided us with small satellite phones issued with very clear instructions that we could talk to our families but only for five minutes per fortnight because of the high cost. I went back to the headquarters staff and highlighted the tremendous dilemma this posed for our contingent. Were we restricted to five minutes every fortnight or could we put credit in the bank and 'break out' once a month and indulge in a ten-minute conversation? For some reason, those back in Australia did not appreciate my caustic humour and somewhat cynical request. In solving this ridiculous dilemma, I resorted to 'channeling' one of General Cosgrove's general philosophies. He was known to be tough but supportive of junior officers. He could be relied upon to have a 'twinkle in the eye' when something irregular was being contemplated. Behind this demeanour was a philosophical conviction: sometimes you are better to beg for forgiveness and just do what is needed. When things were getting ugly and the news emanating from East Timor went from unsettling to distressing, I told the officers to use the phones for as long as they needed to allay the concerns of their families. I was never sent the bill but it would have been high.

When we were able to get back onto the streets we encountered all sorts of messages. The pro-Indonesian militias made no effort to conceal their participation in the wanton destruction of what was formerly Indonesian government property and the wilfil killing of innocent civilians whose actual political allegiances were probably unknown. Figure 12 was one of many threatening messages from the militia leader, Eurico Guterres.

Guterres was the public face of the militia with his long hair, shaded sunglasses and khaki cap. Aged 30 when the ballot was held, his parents were killed by Indonesian forces in 1976 on suspicion of being pro-Fretilin. In 1988, he was arrested for being part of a plot to assassinate President Suharto and then switched sides—from being anti to pro-Indonesian. He then spied on the independence movement until his expulsion in 1990. He was deeply loathed by the independence movement which considered him a traitor to his own people. The message in Figure 12 is loosely translated:

I came carrying the fire of death and I drink the blood of anti-integrationists. Before you enjoy the results of the United Nations and Australia's deceit, I will totally destroy you. Did you think you could have freedom without sacrifice?

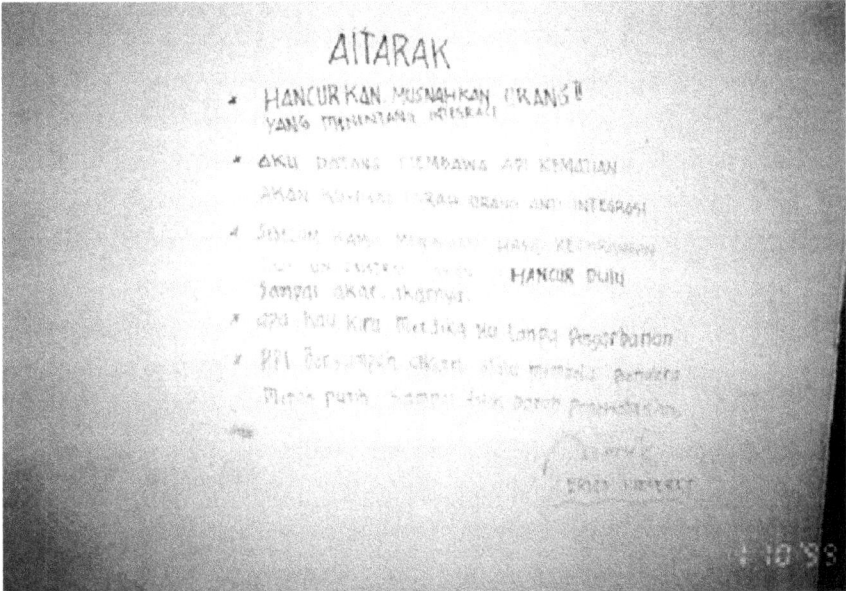

Figure 12:   An open message from militia leader Eurico Guterres

These were not idle threats. He and his followers killed their fellow East Timorese.

Once UNAMET personnel were co-located in the UN compound in Dili, we were faced with serious health and safety problems. A large number of local people were admitted to the compound for their own protection. It soon became apparent in discussions with Ian Martin that an evacuation of UN personnel was important in improving the prospects that an intervention force would be dispatched. Our mandate did not authorise intervention to end the violence and destruction; nor did we have the capability.

There was a strong sense among the mission's leadership that it would be wise for UNAMET to withdraw without delay. Our hearts were with the local people and we did not want to let them down. But our presence was impeding a workable solution to the problem. It was a tremendously difficult and tense time for everyone who participated in the mission. Our work seemed far from over but the deteriorating circumstances dictated that it had to end. The UN Security Council had earlier extended UNAMET's mandate until the end of November 1999 but we were evacuated ahead of INTERFET's arrival on 20 September and commenced our return one week later.

I have drawn four insights from my experience of being in East Timor at a critical time in its history. The first concerns the use of proxy forces. When a nation state relies on proxy forces in pursuit of its national interests, it crosses a very dangerous and unpredictable line. This happened in East Timor. It did not secure the outcome Jakarta wanted and it temporarily diminished Indonesia's standing on the world stage.

My second insight is about the importance of leadership without fanfare. By this I mean leadership that is self-effacing and free of hubris. The Prime Minister, John Howard, provided firm political leadership that focussed on achieving the best outcome for the East Timorese and which quietly enhanced Australia's reputation in the region. Notwithstanding the militia rampage, the ballot was successful and the East Timorese determined their own future. The Prime Minister avoided any hint of triumphalism as he sought to rebuild Australian-Indonesian relations after the most strained period in their recent history. Leadership without fanfare had resolved a long-standing difficulty between the two nations without causing any permanent ill-will between Canberra and Jakarta. In our own quiet way I think UNAMET staff had also exhibited the finest qualities of leadership without fanfare.

My third insight is concerned with caring for those who participate in these deployments when they return home to a society that knows little of what they experienced and which is ill-prepared to assist their reintegration. The deployment was several months in duration; its impact on souls, minds and bodies can persist for decades. Twenty years after our evacuation, I continue to have conversations with individuals who are struggling with the after-effects of what they saw and heard. It is impossible to forget the implosion of an entire society and the widespread abandonment of civilised conduct. Some within the militias engaged in merciless killing sprees that would have extended to UN personnel had fear of the consequences not restrained the worst excesses of human barbarity. We witnessed unmitigated evil and it left an enduring mark on many people. Keeping in touch with people following these types of activities is vitally important. People look to their leaders to initiate such conversations, and to care, well after a mission's formal end is proclaimed.

My fourth insight is very straightforward. I observed the galvanising power of quiet determination. The East Timorese were extraordinary. They touched our hearts and will remain in our memories forever. For every crazed militia member there were many more dignified and noble individuals who refused to respond to violence with violence. They were the same people who led the reconciliation movement that sought to move East Timor from its painful and divided past to a more hopeful and united future.

As General Gordon Sullivan wrote, 'hope is not a method'. After my experience with UNAMET I understood that well. But with conviction, courage and competent people, it is remarkable what can be achieved.

Endnotes

1   My appreciation to a member of my staff, Sam P, who helped with the adaptation of this oral presentation into written form.

2   John McCarthy, 'The Myths of Australia's role in East Timorese independence' at aspistrategist blog, posted 18 January 2020.

3   My appointment was as Chief of Operations of 50 military liaison officers and as national commander of the five Australian Army officers who deployed as part of Rotation One of the United Nations Assistance Mission East Timor (UNAMET) and the incoming Rotation Two officers.

4   https://peacekeeping.un.org/mission/past/unmit/background.shtml

5   The full text of the agreement can be found at: https://www.usip.org/sites/default/files/file/resources/collections/peace_agreements/east_timor_05051999.pdf

CHAPTER 5

UNAMET: a police perspective

Martin Hess

When most Australians recall the events of 1999 in East Timor, they might bring to mind the militia violence in September and perhaps Australia's often turbulent relationship with Indonesia. They will certainly bring to mind the military intervention and the role played by the ADF in restoring law and order ahead of the former Indonesian province's transition to independent nationhood. There is, however, a substantial gap in the collective memory. Most Australians overlook the United Nations Mission in East Timor (UNAMET) preceding the International Force East Timor (INTERFET) deployment, and they are unaware of two decades of continuous and effective police engagement.[1]

UNAMET was the reason INTERFET existed. UNAMET operated between June and September 1999 and secured the ballot of the population which paved the way for eventual independence in 2002. When the ballot result was announced on 4 September 1999,[2] pro-Indonesian militia groups, and elements of Indonesian security forces took reprisals in the form of a scorched earth policy and the forced mass migration of East Timorese to West Timor. These actions forced the evacuation of UNAMET to Darwin. An international military intervention was the only way to restore order.

This chapter reflects on the involvement of the Australian Federal Police (AFP) in UNAMET and in subsequent missions within East Timor.

United National Civilian Police (UNCIVPOL)

An agreement signed on 5 May 1999 placed domestic security responsibility in the hands of the Indonesian Police (POLRI). It had only recently been separated from the military. The Indonesian military, *Tentara Nasional Indonesia* (TNI), retained substantial political power from the Suharto period and resisted attempts to conduct a ballot in East Timor. The TNI also exerted significant influence over POLRI. The TNI also responded by raising several armed militia groups as their proxies to provide plausible deniability for some very violent and hostile activities, aimed at derailing the ballot.

Under the terms of the '5 May Agreement', UN Civilian Police were unarmed. They were deployed in lieu of an international military peacekeeping force because the TNI objected to such a force on Indonesian sovereign territory, especially one led by Australia.[3] Finally, there was an agreement to deploy as many as 280 unarmed UN Civilian Police. The largest single national contingent was provided by the AFP. I was a member of the first 15 AFP members to deploy in mid-June 1999, along with police from New Zealand, Britain, Ireland and Spain, as they became available and arrived in Darwin for on-forwarding to Dili.[4] Upon arrival, we formed electoral teams that consisted of two electoral officers, a driver-interpreter and a UN Civilian Police Officer. We then deployed into regional areas.

In terms of administrative support and medical assistance, there was little of the kind expected in a traditional military mission. There was an extreme risk of death or serious injury from pro-Indonesian militia groups. When this occurred there were no medical facilities and little prospect of evacuation. Nor was there military back up. As the former UN Special Representative for the Secretary General (SRSG) for UNAMET, Ian Martin, observed, these were conditions and circumstances that would not be acceptable today.[5] In many of these areas we were the first Europeans the local people had seen since the Portuguese had departed hastily in 1974. UNAMET was seen by these people as a form of salvation from what had been a cruel occupation by Indonesian forces.

Throughout the entirety of UNAMET, international and locally engaged staff and the local East Timorese population were subject to hostile and violent activities by the pro-Indonesian militia groups. Although UN police were unarmed and placed in harm's way, the AFP members of UNAMET believe they were saved from being targeted and outgunned by the unpredictable thugs in the violent militias in being unarmed. The best defences were the traditional police traits of impartiality, objectivity and an ability to negotiate under pressure. This was a strategy based more on hope than science. Although, in the case of UNAMET it was effective and worked, it should not form a template for deploying civilian police in similar hazardous circumstances or hostile environments.

Militia groups were well armed and supported by elements of the Indonesian security forces, both police and military. Plainly, lightly armed civilian police would have been both outgunned and potentially targets for armed hostility. Being unarmed removed any possible pretext for direct violence on the part of the militia groups claiming self-defence as mitigation for violence against UN Civilian Police. Former AFP Sergeant Don Barnby, a former member of the Australian Special Air Service Regiment and Vietnam veteran, made this clear in a radio interview with ABC Darwin en route to Dili on 24 August 2019.[6] That many of the civilian police in the UNAMET mission came from countries such as New Zealand and the United Kingdom where armed policing is not the norm made deploying unarmed police less politically problematic.[7] The absence of police from these countries would have diminished the credibility and effectiveness of the UN Civilian Police element of UNAMET considerably.

The Militia

There are significant political reasons for downplaying the relationship between the Indonesian security forces and the militia groups. The reluctance to acknowledge this link can only be the subject of guesswork but must include the overriding interests associated with the Australian-Indonesian strategic relationship.[8] While I understand and acknowledge this factor, I invite readers who doubt this formal link to credible accounts produced by the American academic, Geoffrey Robinson,[9] and the Australian academic and former Australian Army Officer, Peter Bartu.[10] Both were part of the UNAMET mission in various capacities. Also relevant is the Chega reconciliation report on the violence.[11] These are credible sources and provide ample evidence of the relationship between the Indonesian military and the pro-Indonesian militia groups.[12]

The Executive Summary of Truth and Reconciliation Commission (CAVR) in 2005 summarises the nature of this relationship:

> The militia groups were formed, armed, funded, directed and controlled by the Indonesian security forces. Indonesian military personnel served as commanders of some militia groups, senior commanders endorsed the militias, they operated from Indonesian military bases, and commonly committed atrocities in the presence of or under the direction of uniformed members of the TNI.
>
> The programme conducted by members of the Indonesian security forces used violence and terror, including killing, torture, beatings, rape and property destruction in an attempt to force East Timorese voters to opt formally to 'integrate' with Indonesia. When this strategy failed to produce the intended result, the security forces and their auxiliaries went on a rampage of violence directed against people and property, and forcibly deported several hundred thousand East Timorese to West Timor.

Robinson (2003) reports that their brutal methods included:

> [T]argeted killing, corpse display and mutilation … and … following standard TNI practice, these were intended to be exemplary - to send a message to others in the community of what would happen to those who did not heed the militias' or the TNI's warnings. The bodies of the victim were often mutilated in some way—decapitated, disembowelled or hacked into small pieces—and then left in full public view.[13]

Voilence erupts

The ballot was delayed until 30 August 1999 due to militia activities, and there was a real risk that voting might be cancelled altogether. Despite extreme intimidation by pro-Indonesian militia groups, the ballot took place on 30 August 1999. On the day, 98.5 percent of courageous and determined registered voters actually expressed their political will. Unexpectedly, 78.5 percent voted against the Indonesian offer of autonomy, preferring the move towards independence which eventuated in 2002.[14] In addition to advising POLRI in relation to the ballot, the role of UN Civilian Police was to secure the ballot material on Polling Day, and ensure it was securely conveyed from remote polling places to the electoral tally room in Dili. This was most often achieved through the use of helicopters.

Ballot boxes with helo Maubisse, 31 August 1999

The UN Compound Dili, 4 September 1999

Throughout the entirely of UNAMET, there were a number of very dangerous incidents. Although they are too numerous to mention, one is worthy of close attention. When the result was announced on 4 September, the territory was quickly engulfed in civil strife in a well-orchestrated campaign of violence, in a scorched earth operation. Many people, UN staff included, evacuated to Dili to a rapidly crowding UN compound and an adjoining school.

On the evening of 5 September 1999, amidst the razing of the central area of Dili, there was at least one machine gun firing at Timorese fleeing in the twilight, up the hills behind the compound, seeking the safety of the mountains. The tracer was clearly evident. There were grenades exploding and small arms fire, some into the UN compound. Someone from the pro-Indonesian side entered the high school next to the UN compound and fired shots from a semi-automatic firearm. This panicked the people who attempted to scale the wall between the school and the UN compound, some throwing

EAST TIMOR TROUBLE SPOTS @ 4th September 1999

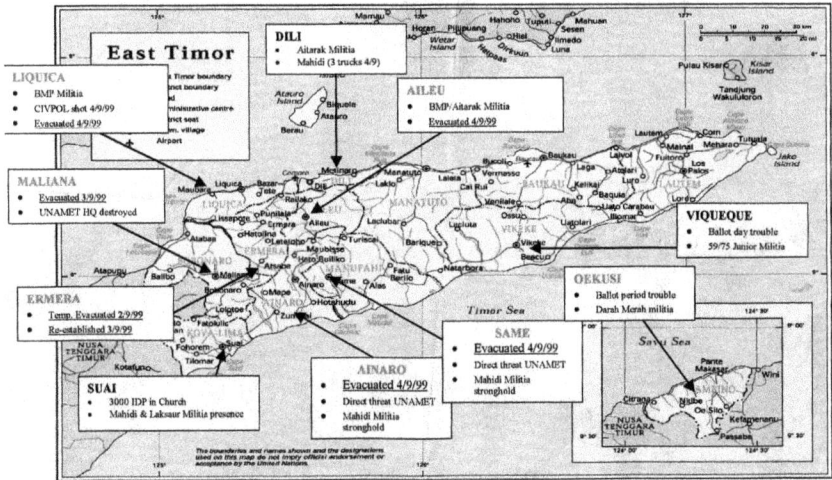

Trouble spots, 04 September 1999

their children over the wall where they became entangled in the razor wire. Eventually the gate between the school and the compound was unlocked by an AFP officer, David Savage.

Those inside the compound, numbering about 500, headed for the auditorium. There there was a great risk of panic, as the lights were lowered to make those there a less obvious target for the machine gunner at the front gate. There was a real fear that those outside the gate might enter the compound or, at least, fire more intentionally into the crowd as some of the militia had been doing sporadically during the afternoon. To settle people down, a young 19-year-old Timorese girl sang *Ave Maria* and said the Lord's Prayer in Tetum. This had the immediate effect of calming clearly distressed people.

Return to Timor Leste August-September 2019

I recently returned to Timor Leste, with a group of my AFP UNAMET colleagues, for the 20th anniversary of UNAMET, and had the privilege of meeting this girl twice through a British UNAMET colleague. Her name is Tata. She is now the deputy head of mission in the Embassy of Timor Leste in Kuala Lumpur.

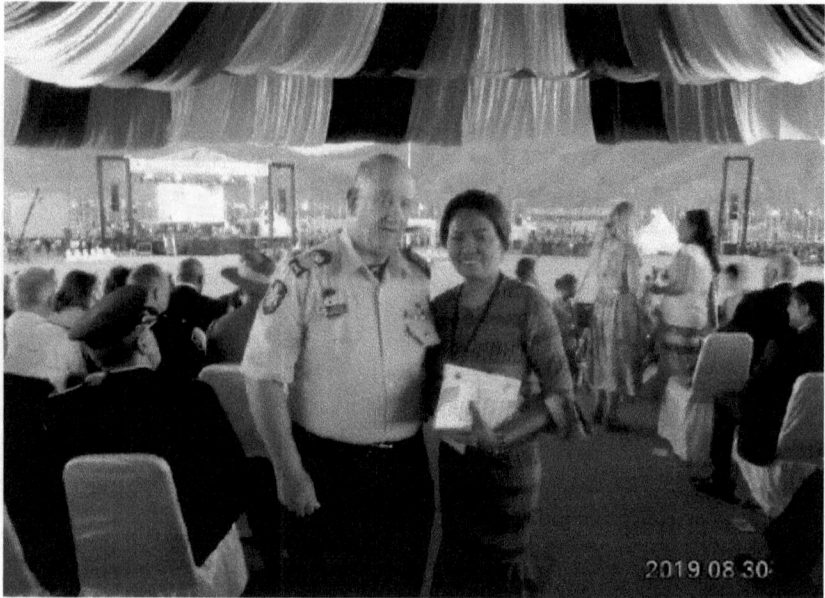

Martin Hess and Tata, Taso Tolu Dili, 30 August 2019

I was also re-acquainted with one of the interpreters, Afonso de Jesus, who had worked at Maubisse with one of the electoral teams. He was evacuated to Australia in September 1999 but later returned to a new life in Timor Leste. In 2002 he joined the newly formed *Policia Nacionale de Timor Leste* (PNTL) and eventually rose through the ranks to become the police Commissioner. He is presently the police attache at the Embassy of Timor Leste in Canberra.[15]

Eventually we were evacuated by various means from Dili to Darwin where life continued as normal. Once safely in Darwin, we arranged to return to our homes. In 2001, the AFP members of UNAMET were awarded a Group Bravery Citation at Government House, Yarralumla. I proudly wore the citation at an Anzac Day commemoration in Canberra when I was approached by a man who wanted to know more about it. After a brief conversation we established that he piloted the RAAF C130 Hercules transport plane that evacuated us from Dili. The C130 was a very welcome sight. As we embarked, we were being watched by some very angry and well-armed Indonesian soldiers who deeply resented our presence on Indonesian territory. I boarded the C130 with a few of my AFP colleagues and two American police officers with whom we had been working. As we were being watched, one

AFP and US UN Civ Pol Dili Airport, 06 September 1999

of these officers, a former Green Beret, Vietnam veteran and New York City police officer, offered me his police shirt. It featured the American flag. He thought it would help because the militias were targeting anyone wearing clothing emblazoned with an Australian flag. I declined. There cannot have been too many occasions in recent diplomatic history when the Australian flag attracted more hostility than the 'Star Spangled Banner'.

Between announcing the ballot result on 4 September and the arrival of INTERFET on 20 September, the militia groups, and some local East Timorese battalions of the TNI, executed a well-planned campaign of pre-meditated and well-targeted violence, killing an estimated 1400 people. Many more were injured or forcibly relocated to the adjoining province of West Timor. There actions were forlorn. The spiteful actions of the TNI and the militias would not reverse the result. The people of East Timor had decided and the road to independence was now open.

UNAMET trendsetting

UNAMET was devised and deployed at relatively short notice. The First AFP contingent was also assembled at short notice and played an instrumental role. Although it was a security failure, UNAMET was an electoral success and a democratic triumph. It was a whole-of-government achievement for Australia. The Australian Electoral Commission (AEC) was integrally involved in designing the ballot.[16] The AFP advised the newly created POLRI in their duties with respect to the ballot. AFP officers secured the ballot boxes to polling places throughout the province and returned them to the central tally room in Dili. Military Liaison Officers were provided by the ADF. A number of other government representatives from agencies such as DFAT, performed various roles. This required a high degree of commitment and coordination at the political level, an essential ingredient in mission success.

Commitment, preferably bi-partisan, at the political level, is vital to the long-term nature of police missions. The Howard Government understood this and demonstrated this commitment throughout its term, particularly with the creation and funding of the AFP International Deployment Group (IDG). There had been other international missions involving the AFP, mostly in distant places where Australia had little or no political 'skin' in the game. UNAMET was different. There was a great deal of political interest and there were domestic, regional and global implications. UNAMET started a trend with follow-on regional police capacity development missions such as the Regional Assistance Mission to the Solomon Islands (RAMSI) in 2003 providing a blue-print for regional interventions. This showed the political courage required to address challenges of a new era, recognising that there were other tools in the international relations tool box besides trade, training, aid and military intervention.

Courage

Individual courage, both physical and moral, is an integral part of mission success. During UNAMET the police displayed both. The AFP Group Bravery Citation states:

> Immediately following the ballot violence broke out and there were many reported killings as East Timor was quickly engulfed in civil strife. Despite the threat to their safety, police members of UNAMET offered protection and refuge to sections of the population targeted by the pro-integration militias and mounted patrols in the surrounding areas which helped reduce fear and tension. In carrying out their policing duties members of UNAMET often placed their own lives at significant risk.[17]

This commendation is reflective of police not only doing the right thing but knowing what constituted the right thing to do. This relates directly to the role the police play domestically as part of the social contract between the citizenry and their government, with the express objective of enhancing and preserving peace, order and good government, none of which was evident in East Timor in 1999.

Police in any society are both security sector and justice sector actors. Over the past two decades the AFP has been integral in regional efforts to enhance the trust of regional communities in their police, and thus enhance the social contract in those countries, within the local cultural context. This sort of approach to development of regional police capacity started in the immediate aftermath of UNAMET.

Peace is not only the absence of conflict. It relies on the presence of justice which is the firmest pillar of good government. Continuity of justice-based efforts underwrites sustainable peace. It is a good form of forward-leaning diplomacy. The AFP has been involved in Timor Leste continuously since mid-June 1999. This involvement has been multi-faceted, involving AFP membership of all the UN missions in Timor and continued after the UN's withdrawal in 2012 with the Timor Leste Police Development Program (TLPDP), which currently has ten AFP members.

Policia Nacional de Timor Leste

A sovereign police force is an attribute of national sovereignty. A police force which can satisfactorily balance its authority with accountability is essential to the health of liberal democracy. The PNTL was formed in 2002, the year that East Timor independence and became Timor-Leste. Shortly after its formation, the PNTL accepted between 600–1000 appropriately vetted former East Timorese members of POLRI without any significant issues.

Members of the PNTL have deployed in small numbers to Kosovo and Guinea Bissau. The UN also sent 90 PNTL to South Sudan. The contingents may be small but the trajectory is clearly upwards in meeting the growing demands of suitably trained and qualified civilian police to address the many and varied issues faced by the international community, including the UN.

Former AFP with PNTL, Gleno, 02 September 2019

PNTL BOP, Dili, 28 August 2019

Continuity of effort: regional police engagement

This AFP line of effort of assisting host nation police continues in regional missions with particular emphasis on the Pacific. There are standing police development missions in Papua New Guinea, the Solomon Islands, Vanuatu, Tonga and Samoa. Samoa is also the home of the Pacific Transnational Crime Network (PTCN) in which the AFP plays a significant role, and which serves Australia's national interests by addressing crime offshore before it reaches Australia, including the trans-Pacific drug trade from the Americas.

After withdrawing from East Timor early in September 1999, the AFP sent a small number of members back to East Timor with INTERFET under the UNAMET mandate. This commitment transitioned to the UNTAET period which began in early 2000.[18] The UN had several different iterations and eventually withdrew in 2012. Each UN mission had AFP members among their members. The AFP remains with a police development program known as the Timor Leste Police Development Program (TLTDP).

The next major international commitment for the AFP followed the al Qaeda attacks on New York and Washington in September 2001. There was an AFP Close Protection Team with Prime Minister Howard in Washington when the terrorists struck. The AFP worked effectively with the United States Secret Service to reunite the prime minister and his wife. Globally-inspired religious terrorism struck closer to home when an Indonesian affiliate of al Qaeda, Jemaah Islamiyah, detonated several bombs in Bali in October 2002, killing 202 people including 88 Australians. The first international approach by POLRI for assistance was to the AFP. This eventuated in a very strong and respectful relationship between the AFP and POLRI which continues to deepen and mature.

In 2003, with a severely deteriorating environment in the Solomon Islands to Australia's near north-east, Prime Minister Howard again called upon the AFP to lead the security reform aspect of a regional intervention which became known as the Regional Assistance Mission to the Solomon Island (RAMSI). RAMSI concluded in 2017 but, like Timor Leste, a follow-on police development programme continues. It is known as the Solomon Islands Police Development Program (SIPDP) and around 45 AFP members are involved in its delivery.

Continuing missions in East Timor and the Solomon Islands required a separate business area within the AFP to support them. The International Deployment Group (IDG) was established in 2004 for this purpose and was expanded in 2006 due to public order incidents in Dili, Honiara and Tonga. The IDG no longer exists as a discrete AFP portfolio and has been combined with the International Operations (IO) portfolio. Under this portfolio, the AFP performs an important role internationally in police capacity development in the Pacific region, police liaison roles in Europe, the Americas, the Middle East, South-East Asia and the South-West Pacific, and in joint task forces combatting child sex tourism, drugs and violent extremism with partner police forces in many places, including both China and the United States.

This international dimension is particularly important given 70 percent of criminal activity targeted by the AFP has offshore origins or links. Strong and trusted relationships with regional police forces are vital to the AFP's role in policing for a safer Australia, as the AFP relies on the rapid transmission of reliable information between trusted partners to fulfil its mandate.

Courage for peace

At the launch of the *Courage for Peace Exhibition* at the Australian War Memorial on 17 October 2019, the Foreign Minister, Senator Marise Payne, remarked:

> Australia has contributed to ... many peacekeeping operations and most of those unarmed ... we don't shrink from the task of bringing peace and saving lives even ... at the risk of our own. Indeed, generations of Australian governments have decided the building of peace is at least as important as the making of war.

> It is both a necessity and a choice for principled nations like Australia to contribute to peace missions ... if we are to live in a rules-based international order where we do not accept that coercion and force dictate the outcomes of disputes; if we choose a world where values and principles are worth defending, and the rights of nations to enjoy prosperity and harmony under international law are paramount; we genuinely believe that inhumanity, genocide, unchecked state-sponsored violence, perpetual instability have no place in the modern world; then

we have no choice but to have the courage to stand up, step forward, share the burden of collective security, regional stability, and breaking the cycle of violence, so that peace has the room to re-establish itself. [19]

Policing and the Rule of Law, domestically, regionally and globally, are very much part of this effort, and the continuous two decades-long engagement between the AFP and the UN and the PNTL in Timor stands as testimony to Australia's and the AFP's commitment to these important principles. This started with UNAMET.

Closing reflections

UNAMET was unique and was the catalyst for all that followed in Timor. Without UNAMET there could not have been a military-led INTERFET, there would have been no follow-on UN missions such as UNTAET, UNMISET, or UNMIT and no TLTDP. There probably would not have been an AFP IDG, and probably no RAMSI, as least in the format which made it so successful. The AFP has now had two decades of continuous engagement in Timor Leste in various capacities, and both countries are the better for it.

A DFAT colleague condensed international interventions into three broad statements: the situation was once bad; Australia helped to address this; Australia is now on good terms with that country. This region was once referred to as the 'arc of instability'. The AFP and various justice programs have made significant contributions to addressing this, and some now refer to it as the 'arc of opportunity'. Timor Leste is a prime example of this conversion from a bad situation, which Australia helped to make better, and despite some political challenges, the police to police relationship between the AFP and the PNTL, and other regional police forces, including POLRI, is strong, respectful and resilient.

The three 'Cs'—Commitment, Courage and the Continuity of Effort—are the three factors which most accurately reflect the legacy of the 20 years since the AFP deployed to East Timor in mid-June 1999. This has yielded dividends, in both the national interest and international good citizenship, by assisting efforts directed at good governance and improved social contracts in the region. This is an important and complementary component of regional initiatives such as the Pacific step-up program in the face of increased strategic competition from powers whose values, particularly in a policing and justice sense, may be somewhat at odds with our own.

Timor-Leste is justified in being proud of its post-independence achievements. Women make up about 40 percent of its parliament. There are 27 embassies in Dili. Timor-Leste is well advanced to join ASEAN and offers a link between ASEAN and Lusophone countries such as Portugal and Brazil. The police force has about 25 percent female members. There are, however, problems looming. Unemployment is serious and there is a significant youth bulge, with 70 percent of the population under 30 years of age. Combined with regional poverty, this provides a potentially volatile threat to future peace and prosperity.

The final observation from my recent visit is that the people of Timor Leste are more confident and much happier than when I was there 20 years ago. There is a general vibrancy about the place, but there is still dire poverty, particularly in the regional, remote and rural areas. Like many similar places, people say that education is the answer. This is partially true. The real answer lies in addressing youth unemployment. The solution requires investment-based economic activity. Attracting foreign and domestic capital, infrastructure and expertise will only come with enhanced stability and security, both of which are being largely addressed through complementary police capacity development and justice programs, in which both the community and the government have a significant stake.

Endnotes

1   For a more complete explanation of AFP involvement in UNAMET see:
    David Savage, *Dancing with the Devil: A Personal Account of Policing the East
    Timor Vote for Independence* (2002) Monash University Press; Martin Hess in
    John Blaxland (ed.), East *Timor Intervention A Retrospective on INTERFET*,
    Melbourne University Press 2015 and Martin Hess, *Submission in response
    to the Foreign Affairs, Defence and Trade Committee request for veteran input
    into the Australian Veteran's Covenant Bill 2019*. Foreign Affairs, Defence and
    Trade Committee Department of the Senate Parliament House Canberra ACT
    2600. file:///C:/Users/Martin%20Hess/AppData/Local/Packages/Microsoft.
    MicrosoftEdge_8wekyb3d8bbwe/TempState/Downloads/Sub%2010%20Dr%20
    Hess%20(1).pdf.

2   98.5 percent of registered voters actually voted, of which 78.5 percent voted
    against the Indonesian offer of autonomy.

3   There were, however, a number of Military Liaison Officers (MLOs), including a
    number from the ADF.

4   Many other nations, including the United States, Malaysia and the Philippines,
    also contributed police members as they became available. Some left other
    missions in places such as Kosovo to join UNAMET.

5   Ian Martin, former UN SRSG to UNAMET: *Speech at UN House*, Dili, 26 August
    2019

6   Steer, A. (ABC Darwin): *They voted yes, knowing they would be killed*. Radio
    Interview: Don Barnby, Martin Hess and David Savage, ABC Darwin, 24 August
    1999: Broadcast Mon 2 Sep 2019, 9:30am https://www.abc.net.au/radio/darwin/
    programs/mornings/timor-afp/11470794.

7   The New Zealand Police members deployed to UNAMET were all members of the
    Armed Offenders Squad.

8   It is noteworthy that there is a continuing discussion concerning publication
    of the Australian War Memorial's Official History of ADF involvement in
    East Timor for fear that it may offend Indonesian sensitivities. This is the
    subject of media reporting: See Paul Daley, 'Australia's history with East Timor
    isn't pretty but it must be told truthfully', *Guardian Australia*, 13 November
    2019: https://www.theguardian.com/australia-news/postcolonial-blog/2019/
    nov/13/australias-history-with-east-timor-isnt-pretty-but-it-must-be-told-
    truthfully?CMP=Share_AndroidApp_News_eed&fbclid=IwAR08eUqvpXYGXyH
    5BZ6klo7f6dLvQY6Qds0GtTb7qkCtsUrJ8aS5Ep3DFNM

9   Geoffrey Robinson, *East Timor 1999: Crimes against Humanity: A Report
    Commissioned by the United Nations Office of the High Commissioner for Human
    Rights (OHCHR)*. University of California Los Angeles, July 2003.

10 Peter Bartu, 'The Militia, the Military, and the People of Bobonaro District',
    Bulletin of Concerned Asian Scholars, Vol. 32, Nos. 1 and 2 (2000), pp. 35–42.

11 *Chega! The Report of the Commission for Reception, Truth and Reconciliation in Timor Leste (CAVR)*. 2005 The systematic programme of violations in 1999. https://www.etan.org/news/2006/cavr.htm.

12 Additionally, the UN Serious Crimes Unit conducted a five-year investigation and found that Indonesian military, police and civil administration were actively involved in the violence and many, including those at the highest levels were indicted for these activities. Most of these indictments quietly lapsed.

13 Robinson, para. 4.3.

14 Many of these voters arose very early in the morning and walked great distances to cast their vote (author's observation). In an age where democracy is subject to increased criticism, this is a salutary lesson for those who doubt the power and determination of those denied a stake in their own political destiny.

15 Both of these people were in the UN Compound on the evening of 5 September 1999 and these two examples epitomise what East Timor was in 1999 and what Timor Leste is in 2019.

16 See M Maley in John Blaxland (ed.), 2015.

17 *Group Bravery Citation*: Australian Federal Police members of UNAMET 1999.

18 The UN Transitional Authority (UNTAET) was established on 25 October 1999 established as a Transitional Authority to administer the Territory, exercise legislative and executive authority during the transition period and support capacity-building for self-government. In a policing sense UNTAET was an Executive Policing mission, whereby UN Police actually enforced the criminal law.

19 Marise Payne, *The Courage for Peace* exhibition launch: Senator the Hon. Marise Payne, Minister for Foreign Affairs and Minister for Women. Australian War Memorial, Canberra, 17 October 2019 https://www.awm.gov.au/commemoration/speeches/senatormarisepayne.

CHAPTER 6

The commander's perspective

Peter Cosgrove

As the commander of the International Force East Timor (INTERFET) I will examine the military aspects of both the deployment and its conduct, with special emphasis on outcomes and learnings which have helped shape the ADF's future structure, doctrine and employment. While the INTERFET operation was comparatively short and relatively bloodless, in many ways it created for the Army an oppportunity for operational and cultural renaissance. While Navy and Air Force both performed superbly, here too one might say that there was a sort of renaissance, particularly in the matter of joint operations at long arm's reach—something we now see as absolutely vital for credible defence posture in our region.

We had a command and control structure before and during INTERFET which I would describe as 'cautiously experimental'. At the apex was the Chief of the Defence Force who had command of all Australian military forces, under the direction of the Commonwealth Government. That is still the case. Supporting him as a staff was a small joint element at Russell Offices in Canberra under a 2-star officer. That 2-star reported directly to the Chief of the Defence Force. The CDF also received detailed technical and operational employment advice from the Service chiefs. This had been the case for a number of years but the experimental part of my earlier remark was that a relatively new construct was a joint headquarters co-located in Sydney with Maritime headquarters. This joint headquarters was known as Headquarters Australian Theatre (HQAST), another 2-star headquarters which had its own substantial intelligence staff. The Commander AST was intended to exercise command over deployed elements, where there was an operational mission to be accomplished (although some operations which were specific to a 'domain' and were still commanded by that service(that is, land, maritime and aerospace). The COMD AST had immediate access to the 'domain' or 'environmental' commanders (Maritime Command, Land Command and Air Command), all of whom were located in or near Sydney.

Finally, the other joint operational entity was my alternate role as Commander of the Deployable Joint Force Headquarters which was the HQ upon which HQ INTERFET was based. It was set upon the Army's headquarters 1st Division, located in Brisbane. This was really a headquarters in waiting, with an outline organisational diagram which showed the presence of maritime and air component headquarters (these maritime and air components ordinarily operated day-to-day with a skeleton staff, beefed up for internal and wider training in an exercise environment). As the name implied, it was thought that this headquarters during time of need would deploy forward to command an operational force, probably offshore in our region. It was envisaged that it would have a land-centric area of operations and that maritime and air assets under its control would probably only be those intimately operating in that area of operations (AO). While some maritime and air assets would move in and out of tactical control, equally, once they departed the AO, these sorts of elements would revert to higher headquarters. Further, it was possible that this joint headquarters would operate as a 'combined' headquarters, that is, taking on (under some level of control) coalition forces.

This system separated the day-to-day exercise of operations from the policy development and practical administration conducted by the ADF and the Department of Defence in Canberra. Detaching strategic and political direction from operational decision-making seems to make sense but does not take into account what we saw in INTERFET (a large, remote force working in a single theatre of operations) and the great diversity and immediacy of military communications and mass media. To put it brutally, HQ AST was, from the first deployments of INTERFET, bypassed in terms of operational information and decisions. It was, however, thoroughly exploited and relied upon in terms of logistics and operational support. Since that time the ADF moved quite swiftly to create a new senior structure for command and control, headquarters joint operations command with a facility at Bungendore, a short drive from Canberra. Day-to-day operations are under the control of a 3-star officer with a large headquarters. This returns the immediacy of information and consultation to the CDF and, thus, to the Government. Before we had the facility at Bungendore, when I was CDF for a while, I used the Vice Chief of the Defence Force as a chief of joint operations. The moment Bungendore was established and operating, appointing a separate commander at the 3-star level was the logical way to go.

Whereas my earlier remark was about capability needing to be enhanced by doctrine—a different command and control arrangement, here I want to remark about the pointers INTERFET gave us in intelligence, surveillance and reconnaissance and some practical learnings about our logistic arrangements. Basil Liddell Hart in his decades of writing about military conflict gave us the term 'the other side of the hill'. In this evocative phrase he was referring to the eternal passion of the military commander to know what was happening that would affect his force and his mission, that was happening out of his view, masked by distance, inter-visibility, subterfuge or lack of attention. At the higher levels of intelligence, we were always well served. Our technical intelligence was sufficient—I do not believe we gained very much in this regard from INTERFET's time in theatre. What was very evident was the great addition to situational awareness for ground troops, call it combat intelligence we would have gained—the value of UAVs, already fielded by other military forces. The ability to loiter, surveil, stare and transmit data remote from the recipient would have been most useful during INTERFET, especially within a concept of a 'pyramid' of airborne surveillance assets. I like to think that the absence of this obvious asset, enlarged our appetite and hastened our acquisition of a growing UAV sensor capability.

Logistics

It has been largely a canard that our logistics nearly or actually 'broke' in East Timor—a sort of 'for want of a nail a kingdom was lost!' We did not do too badly on only several weeks' notice deploying and supplying what ultimately was a force which looked like an Army Division moving through points of entry that looked like the port and airport of Coffs Harbour! There were vulnerable times and inevitably the need for workarounds. Our logisticians performed wonders and gained marvellous experience that has stood the ADF in great stead in the last 20 years. One might say from the INTERFET experience that logistic capability at arm's reach very much informed the major acquisitions of large amphibious and logistic shipping by the Royal Australian Navy and C-17s by the Royal Australian Air Force, both highly capable and highly flexible force elements for projecting and sustaining military operations remote from our forward bases in Australia. While there were, no doubt, many doctrinal, structural adjustments made within the ADF's broad logistic elements which started then and have never stopped in the last 20 years, those two major takeaways from INTERFET, ships and aircraft, stand out.

Command and control

I have already observed that the ADF's joint command structure was somewhat 'experimental' in 1999. A major accomplishment of the preparation and conduct of INTERFET was the enormous 'cultural' progress made at many levels within the three services in terms of recognition and understanding of the peculiarities, needs and capacities of three services in the three operational domains. Two decades on, young men and women who worked together as naval lieutenant equivalents are now star-ranked officers and still working together. Although I retired from the ADF in 2005, in my most recent incarnation as Governor General I have had the opportunity to observe this cultural factor. It has created a wholly advantageous joint environment which sets the ADF in the front rank of nations seeking to exploit the synergies which are now natural to us. There are several great contributors to this outcome: the ADF Academy and its partnership with UNSW, the Command and Staff College, the Centre for Defence and Strategic Studies, many other ADF training courses and, naturally, the joint headquarters and staff branches in the Department of Defence. It might be said that with our comparatively modest personnel numbers, we are in a 'sweet spot' for this cultural factor to be so important. To me, in relation to INTERFET, we did not invent a new set of arrangements upon which to nuture a nascent culture. We employed and then enhanced the existing arrangements and demonstrated the importance of the joint 'spirit' as an integral part of our national capability.

External relationships

The ADF enjoys military relationships around the world. From the earliest days of our military history as Federated Commonwealth, we have built on close relationships with our British mentors, our New Zealand cousins, our American friends and, episodically, with other militaries. Australia is now an international player, not least in the security area. This level of familiarity is wide and becoming even wider. Beyond these kindred nations, our relationship with the Indonesian military has been a complex one for obver five decades. The relationship has sometimes been quite inimical, often cordial and always attentive. Before and during INTERFET, it might be said that the relationship dial had moved towards the left. Yet, and perhaps unsurprisingly, part of my mantra to all Australian force elements and, indeed, to our coalition partners, was that our job in East Timor was threefold: first, to restore and maintain peace and security for East Timor; second, to assist the United Nations to return and perform its functions in East Timor (this included establishing a follow-on UN military force); and, third and emphatically, to improve our relationships with Indonesia. I was acknowledging that this area of work required more than lip service.

How, then, did we go? Many more books will be written on Australian-Indonesian relations at the end of the twentieth century but I believe they will all conclude that we were diligent and determined to repair whatever had been broken in 1998–99 and to build fresh partnerships for a new millennium. The Australian unit and sub-unit commanders in East Timor were left in no doubt that our relationship with Indonesia is never a temporary novelty. It is a perpetual reality which will exceed all our lifetimes.

The proof of the pudding came later. After a few more bumps in the road (for example, the Bali and Jakarta terrorist attacks and the criminal cases involving the 'Bali Nine' drug smugglers), Australia's response to the 2004 tsunami which devastates large parts of Indonesia, prompted a stunning outpouring of public sympathy and government support. The Australian character was seen in its very best light. It might have *persona non grata* as a military leader in the archipelago after 1999 but, in the near aftermath of the tsunami and Australia's generous response, I was warmly welcomed to Jakarta. Soon after the crash of the Navy Seaking helicopter 'Shark 02' on the Indonesian island of Nias, President Yudhoyono visited Australia and stood at the foot of the caskets of the nine ADF who had died in his homeland and paid his nation's respect, honouring their memory with an Indoensian medal. That was a sign to me that the relationship, military-to-military, was restored. An example of the quiet pathway to continued understanding is the 'Ikahan program'. Usually retired ADF and TNI officers together with other experts engage in a second-track dialogue, alternating the venue between the two nations to discuss shared issues and outward-looking perspectives. As Governor-General, I was a strong proponent of this program and my successor is similarly supportive. Indeed, he has committed himself to learning Bahasa at UNSW Canberra alongside defence Academy officer cadets. As with most of our other bilateral relations, there should be no comfortable assumptions about the need for sensitivity, vigour, understanding and compromise in our relationship with Indonesia. It should always proceed on the basis that we need each other and there is no end to that need.

The United Nations

Before INTERFET, Australia had a splendid peacekeeping service record with the UN. This assessment goes back to the UN's earliest days when our peacekeepers, generally in small groups, worked under its flag. In Korea, we fought directly under the benediction of the UN. In more recent times, in Namibia and then Cambodia, our people did extraordinarily well. Less widely applauded were UN-mandated interventions in former Yugoslavia and in Rwanda. The UN Security Council resolution 1264 for the intervention in East Timor took us on a new path where the intervention force was empowered to 'take all necessary steps' to restore peace and security to East Timor. There is no immodesty in acknowledging that the UN was relieved and uplifted that the mission was accomplished swiftly and without substantial loss of life, and that East Timor was moved quickly to nationhood. So, in the sense of statecraft, politics, national determination and military outcomes I believe our stocks within the United Nations remain very high. Like all developed countries with a sound economy and a stable, pluralistic government, we get our share of criticism from the international community for our attitude to the UN. Among the 'lifters and leaners', however, all nations would place us in the former category. This perception was not created by INTERFET. It was an outcome and it has been heavily underscored since then.

I will conclude with a few other insights and challenges which were discovered or reinforced by INTERFET. Let me categorise them: leadership of a coalition; managing within a coalition; and, levels of force.

Coalition leadership

Leadership of a coalition is understandably much more complex than command of a unified force. Not only is it necessary to ensure that missions attempted are attainable and acceptable within the force but that, to the degree possible, the coalition commander and staff acknowledge the reality that coalition members are somewhere between elements indisputably under command and 'stakeholders' continually applying local and national interests and influences to their contributions and investments. There is very definitely a twin track nature to the conduct of operations by coalitions: first, the rigorous, professional, military decisions about needs and responses; and, secondly, the art of reasonable and attainable burden sharing within the coalition (and crucially the way any of this will be digested in coalition members' home nations). Australia went into the RAMSI mission in August 2003 in an 'eyes wide open' manner that was informed by the INTERFET experience. In my view, the immediate and continuing success of that mission was proof that Australia is both comfortable and competent in the role of coalition leader. A cautionary note is that higher levels of conflict will test coalitions and, not least, their leaders whenever and wherever that is the case. But the ADF, the Department of Foreign Affairs and Trade and other government agencies are all the better for these experiences of the last 20 years.

Managing in a coalition

Management is very much a subset of leadership. If leadership has much of art, inspiration and emotion, then managing is much more about reason, structure and technique. Managing within a coalition has similar elements of managing within a joint force. It requires diligence and an unending determination to understand and embrace the needs and differences of the coalition membership. Within INTERFET it became an ordinary but important staff function on a daily basis to monitor and work upon relations between Australia and its coalition partners (obviously, because we were the leader) and often between coalition partners to ensure harmony and alleviate or avoid misunderstandings. With our leadership of RAMSI this was a natural role. Again, I am not implying that INTERFET invented this method but it came naturally from the outset in the Solomon Islands. Some coalition partners came to INTERFET naturally and almost inevitably because of their relationship with Australia and/or Indonesia and/or East Timor (our Kiwi cousins would see themselves in one of these baskets). Others came because their nations are prolific supporters of the UN's peacekeeping ventures. Others quite possibly came for reasons unique to the situation and the moment. In any event, they were all very diverse both socially, culturally and politically and in terms of military capacity and ethos.

I took the view that while the mission must come first, last and always, part of my duty was to ensure that each participant in INTERFET felt valued at the end of our mission, whether they were going home or staying on for UNTAET, the follow-on blue beret operation. This meant more than passive overwatch of their welfare and activities but vigorous encouragement for them to bring special skills in to play. For example, the Philippines Army detachment had a medical clinic capability supported by general-purpose troops. They generously proposed to conduct an animal husbandry course for East Timorese farmers in their rural area of operations. I encouraged their initiative. Similarly, the Thai troops engaged in some marvellous public health education programs in and around Dili at a time when the public health system was struggling to re-establish itself under broader UN arrangements. In this way, burden sharing can be expressed and experienced way beyond the point of the bayonet. For me, it was a revelation of the most pleasant kind to see military forces profoundly engaged in these 'nation-building' efforts.

As a postscript to this commentary on coalition management, it is fundamental that coalition forces must always be seen as under the command of, and operating to, the national policies of their home nation. They are 'given on loan' to the coalition and the coalition commander. For operational employment, for discipline, for deployment they remain under their national commander on the ground and fundamentally their parent nation. If the coalition leader and all the other intermediaries remember that as a guide to attitudes and behaviour, it is more likely that the coalition will flourish. That said. I had no doubt that if security challenges had become serious, we had the troops and the leaders to deal with whatever stood before us.

Levels of force

INTERFET had a very powerful mandate. In many ways this simplified our attitudes to rules of engagement (ROE) and eased the stresses associated with consequent planning. For young commanders and soldiers, it meant that in their back pocket was the obligation to apply lethal force if there was no alternative. With that set as the base, it was so much easier to work back towards the 'least violent' resort in achieving the peace and security at every level, which was our goal. Soldiers who know that, if the situation demands, they can apply lethal force are so much more persuasive and intimidating towards having their way without actually ever having to use the lethal sanction. There were some extraordinary challenges to the judgement, courage and forbearance of INTERFET soldiers—perfectly entitled to believe that an imminent threat existed and, therefore, perfectly entitled to use lethal force to defend themselves and their colleagues. Yet, they refrained from firing and managed the threat. Training takes you just so far. Ultimately, individual courage and sound judgement explains why and how bloodshed was avoided. What is the abiding lesson? If you have good troops (which we did), you can have powerful ROE which allow you ultimately to compel an outcome. When conveyed with determination to a potential adversary, you become very persuasive. We took a different approach to RAMSI. ROE were more restrictive than in East Timor. It was, however, a different situation and adjustments were necessary. We were confident rather than uncertain, due to our INTERFET experience, that the mandated use force had been accurately correlated against the potential threat.

I finish with a few summary remarks about our relationship with Timor-Leste in light of the Australian-led INTERFET intervention. The most important factor upon which to reflect is the 'effluxion of time'. Two decades after the death and destruction of 1999, Timor-Leste is a small nation which is also a close neighbour and a friend. It is important to Australia, as are all of our neighbours. There is no sense of there being a permanent obligation which is prior, more pressing or less pragmatic than that which we have with other nearer neighbours, such as Papua New Guinea. Commander of the 1st Division in 1998, I controlled a post-Tsunami relief operation in the northern regions of New Guinea. We had a poster made. It became emblematic of the wonderful work being done by our surgical and medical teams at Vanimo on New Guinea's north coast. It showed a fuzzy wuzzy angel in a lap lap leading a blinded Australian digger down the Kokoda track. Underneath this well-known photo was a post-tsunami photo of two Aussie military medics kneeling beside a stretcher with a child victim of this terrible disaster. In the background was a RAAF Caribou aircraft. The caption above the photo, written in English and in Pidgin, was 'We will always remember"; the caption below the photograph announced, 'We will always be there'.

This image says it all for East Timor and for our other beloved neighbours in our region. It conveyed a powerful and heartfelt message to Indonesia in 2004. It will promote the same sentiment again wherever we are needed. East Timor and the INTERFET operation was a watershed moment for Australia and for the ADF. From my perspective as the subsequent Chief of the Army and then the Chief of the Defence Force, it was a renaissance. The men and women of the ADF affirmed that they were worthy successors to those who had gone before and were the future leaders of the magnificent men and women who wear our uniform today.

CHAPTER 7

The maritime perspective

James Stapleton

E ach of the three services could learn a great deal from the Australian Defence Force's role in the East Timor intervention. That this operation is usually referred to as an 'intervention' is noteworthy on its own because it encompasses a range of possible activities that rarely receive the attention their importance and the subtlety deserve. When armed force is involved, the very broad concept of an intervention includes many levels of warfare. When the International Force East Timor (INTERFET) Maritime Forces departed for East Timor in September 1999, the threat to the safety and well-being of Australia's personnel and assets was assumed to be real. Notwithstanding the Indonesian Government's acceptance of an international force to restore order in East Timor, the Australian Government was unable to predict how the Indonesian military would respond to an international maritime presence on the shores of what continued to be its 27th province. The readiness levels of the deployed ships were certainly well beyond the standard peacetime Minimum Level of Capability (MLOC). Further, the ADF's resources were stretched in the maritime arena. There was no reserve or surge capacity should it be needed.

The maritime component of the newly established Deployable Joint Force Headquarters (DJFHQ (M)) had been established at Maritime Headquarters (MHQ) in Sydney in January 1999. Late in August of that year, a small planning team moved to Brisbane to join DJFHQ, an Army organisation that later formed the core of INTERFET's Joint and Combined Task Force

Headquarters. The task of the maritime element was to assist with the development of *Operation Spitfire* which was a Services Assisted Evacuation (SAE) of United Nations and Australian personnel attached to the United Nations Mission East Timor (UNAMET) who remained in Dili. The bulk of the naval component moved from Sydney to Brisbane on 7 September 1999 and thereafter became the Naval Component Command (NCC) under the INTERFET Commander, Major General Peter Cosgrove.

Integration of the planning teams presented challenges. This was not unexpected given the arrangements were new and untested. The naval component was initially seen as 'just an add-on' to the DJFHQ. Although some of the people had worked together before, there was a brief period of confusion about roles, responsibilities and reporting. The lack of clarity was quickly overcome by the senior leadership. The naval component was soon fully integrated despite the existence of long-standing cultural differences between the Navy and the Army. It was also apparent that the naval and military components had only a slight knowledge of what each brought to operational planning. The team melded into a cohesive and cooperative group that was able to draft the plans needed to manage a highly fluid operational situation.

A maritime concept of operations was hastily developed despite planners not knowing what the final composition of maritime assets that would be available for the operation. The principal objective of the NCC was to support the land forces in achieving their goals. In brief, the maximum combat force needed to be deployed in the minimum time. There was an expectation from the Australian Government and the international community that the INTERFET deployment would involve a substantial on-the-ground presence in East Timor. To this end, early maritime planning focused on conducting area surveillance, protecting the sea lines of communication to East Timor and providing the necessary sea lift assets to move and sustain the land force which consisted of troops and heavy equipment. Sustaining the deployed force was the most difficult issue facing planners. From an RAN perspective, the most significant shortcoming was in heavy sea lift. Simply, we did not have enough ships. Delays in the modernisation of two ex-United States Navy amphibious transport ships (USS *Fairfax County* and USS *Saginaw* which had become HMA ships *Manoora* and *Kanimbla*) meant that the

5791-ton Landing Ship Helicopter (LSH) HMAS *Tobruk* was the only heavy lift capability available from the outset. There were also three Landing Craft Heavy (LCHs) HMA Ships *Balikpapan*, *Brunei* and *Labuan*. They were much smaller vessels (displacing 517 tons when fully loaded) but would be available to support the land force as required.

The Navy had recently commissioned a new ship, HMAS *Jervis Bay*, a 86-metre wave piercing catamaran fast ferry, which was chartered directly from the builder and based in Darwin. *Jervis Bay* was capable of sailing the 430 nautical miles between Darwin to Dili in just 11 hours at an average speed of 45 knots. As the ship's fuel tanks had been enlarged, she had a range of 1000 nautical miles and would not need to refuel in Dili. The vehicle ramp had been augmented to make it self-deployable and the vehicle deck reinforced to accommodate heavy trucks and other bulky equipment. *Jervis Bay* proved her worth time and again. Even with *Jervis Bay*, the Navy simply did not have the strategic lift capability necessary to support operations ashore. This shortfall was overcome with merchant ships that were contracted to transport the land force's heavy equipment to Dili—a city with limited infrastructure and a barely adequate wharf. Other highly capable sea lift platforms would arrive later in the operation. From October-November they include RSN *Excellence* and RNS *Intrepid* from Singapore, *Siroco* and *Jacques Cartier* from France and ITS *San Giusto* from Italy. Critical fuel support was supplied by the tankers HMAS *Success*, HMNZS *Endeavour* and HMCS *Protecteur*. Several United States Navy tankers, *Kilauea*, *San Jose* and *Tippecanoe*, were also deployed to the area of operations and assisted when possible.

In all, 10 nations eventually provided ships to the INTERFET intervention. Australia naturally provided the largest number of naval assets with 14 ships deployed to East Timor between the start of the operation on 20 September 1999 until its conclusion on 23 February 2000. The RAN ships mentioned earlier were completed by the frigates *Adelaide*, *Anzac*, *Darwin*, *Newcastle* and *Melbourne*; the American cruiser *Mobile Bay* and the amphibious assault ships *Belleau Wood*, *Peleliu* and *Juneau*; the British destroyer *Glasgow*; New Zealand frigates *Te Kaha* and *Canterbury*; the Portuguese frigate *Vasco da Gama*; and the Royal Thai Navy landing ship *Surin*. My reflections on the important lessons and the enduring legacies of the INTERFET operation from a maritime perspective can be grouped under a number of themes: national reputation, regional engagement and relationships, readiness, interoperability and command and control, and capability improvements.

ADF reputation (and HQADF command structure)

The success of Operation *Stabilise* enhanced Australia's standing in the community of nations and bolstered the ADF's reputation nationally and internationally. The deployment raised the ADF's profile in the eyes of the government and the Australian public. There was some uncertainty about the ADF's capacity to accomplish the operation objectives given that Australia was the chief contributor and the lead nation rather than filling its more familiar role of being a junior partner. International and regional respect were also enhanced as the operation proceeded swiftly and successfully, demonstrating a capability to lead, plan, mount and execute a coalition military operation that was important to the future of the Asia-Pacific region.

Confidence within the coalition and across the ADF grew as the operation progressed and the contributing nations came together. The management of the coalition was one of the most important tasks for Australian commanders at all levels. The experience gained by the ADF in the management of this particular coalition led to changes in day-to-day HQADF command arrangements which now seem more streamlined to encompass force capability and joint planning. There was duplication and confusion in the INTERFET command structure within HQADF as the new operational level headquarters located in Sydney (COMAST) was also trialed. While the direct military link to international forces was at the strategic level in Canberra, implementation and integration remained at the operational level. Political considerations also influenced activity at the operational level. In sum, there were too many levels of command producing too much complexity in securing decisions. The new HQADF organisation appears to better meet the requirements of all levels—tactical, operational and strategic—including consideration of political imperatives and limitations and the handling of national requirements for any international forces assigned to the operation. INTERFET was new ground for the ADF and Australia at all levels. Much was learned and much was changed.

Regional / international military relationships

Regional and International military relations remain an important cornerstone of Australia's defence and security. Shared equipment (where nationally acceptable), common doctrine and joint training all contribute to the cohesion of future coalitions and the effective integration of forces. Interactions between navies has been a common thread of history, enabling maritime forces who share doctrine and procedures to integrate quickly into a cohesive and responsive force. INTERFET was very much a joint and a combined force. General Cosgrove was unequivocal in acknowledging that 'the naval presence was not just a nice to have add-on ... [it is] an important indicator of international resolve and most reassuring to all of us who rely on the sea lifeline'. The ability to come together quickly as a cohesive entity to deliver potent force is largely due to the maintenance of maritime relationships and the fine-tuning of shared doctrines and protocols at both an international and a regional level. INTERFET's maritime forces were a major deterrent to any potential enemy at sea and a demonstration of international and regional resolve in support for East Timor. The capability, responsiveness and flexibility of the coalition's naval assets ensured that INTERFET could operate in a secure environment ashore and receive the necessary logistic support to conduct operations.

Building on the experiences of 1999–2000, navies within the region continue to participate in multilateral and unilateral exercises at sea and ashore. The aim is to maintain the interoperability and connection that will be important in any future regional crisis, whether humanitarian or military. Australia's international exercise programmes and practical engagements ensures the ADF remains acquainted with new technologies and emerging capabilities as well as sharing new approaches to fighting at sea. It remains important for an island nation like Australia to stay connected and be a reliable and trusted alliance partner. The challenge remains sharing necessary information between the participating nations within the constraints of multilateral security agreements and regional treaties.

Readiness

Any force's readiness for operations is directly related to the quality of the intelligence upon which it relies. Who is the most pressing adversary? What weapons are they likely to use? How will they secure a tactical advantage? INTERFET's maritime forces were at a higher than usual state of readiness due to recent multinational exercises held in the region. In some respects, the Australian navy was ready for INTERFET. For some months there were indications that there might be a collapse of civil order followed by a humanitarian crisis in East Timor. The possibility of violence after the independence ballot was assessed as being somewhere between likely and inevitable. Without wanting to create a self-fulfilling prophecy, the ADF had been planning and preparing for some involvement in East Timor from early 1999. A number of capability shortfalls had been identified (most notably in sea lift) while deployment programs were adjusted to ensure ships remained in the region—just in case.

But the situation in East Timor deteriorated much more rapidly than anticipated and the decisions of the United Nations, mainly UN Resolution 1264, and Indonesian responses at both the political and military levels created more urgent demands than were originally anticipated. A series of options culminating in a multinational coalition and an INTERFET-style intervention with Australia as the lead nation developed very quickly. It was difficult to know what would be needed and when. Australia had a limited timeframe in which to respond as civilians were being killed and infrastructure was being destroyed. The difficulty of being confident about 'what' and 'when' is common to many military conflicts and bedevils long term planning and preparation. A nation can never be fully prepared for every contingency, however likely or unlikely. It needs to rely on the flexibility of its forces to adapt to changing circumstances. Once the decision to proceed with the INTERFET option was made, military planning and force development proceeded at an incredible pace. When compared with other UN responses to crises in the 1990s, the INTERFET deployment was remarkable, not least the speed with which it was mounted followed by its clear and unqualified success.

The level of readiness maintained by a segment of a nation's forces needs to be high when it comes to fundamental skills in all modes of warfare. This level of readiness provides the capability needed for a response at short notice. It has been said that 'you join the fight the way you are dressed'. There is little time and scarce opportunity to start from basics. INTERFET's maritime assets were a multinational force which together had the appropriate capabilities to meet present and evolving needs of a deteriorating security situation. Monitoring readiness for responding to short notice operations is a vital discipline. This discipline requires constant review of both the strategic situation and the roles assigned to the forces that could be employed in the potential area of operations. This was another important lesson learned from 1999.

Interoperability and command and control

Interoperability at a national and international level between all arms of service is a crucial element of contemporary warfare. In the maritime domain, there are shared naval tactical and procedural doctrines and common maritime warfare publications. At the national level there are Australian Joint Tactical Publications and doctrines which are used for planning and war fighting. These publications have served Australia well both nationally and internationally. The equipment the Navy uses is also interoperable—sometimes. A shared operational awareness and common tactical picture reduces confusion and limit opportunities for 'blue on blue' engagements in which we engage our friends rather than our adversaries. As explained earlier, there is a conflict between the need to share information and the security constraints of existing agreements. This can and must be managed.

Security plays a crucial role in the transfer of information and INTERFET forces were not all cleared to receive the same level of information. This inconsistency further complicated command and control of maritime assets. The command and control challenge reflected the diverse standing of the participating nations and the primacy of their own national objectives which they naturally pursued. A special INTERFET maritime communications group was established to support conveying the right message to the right unit at the right time. There will always be a need for special communications between nations, services and commands when conducting multinational operations. The highly pressing nature of this need was apparent to all participants in 1999. These capabilities have since been included in the ADF's standing capability developments.

Capability improvements

The major maritime shortfall during the INTERFET period of operations was the availability of sealift capability. Acquiring the best ships and arranging for them to be fitted with the right equipment involves a considerable investment of time, thought and money. It took some years for the Australian Government to make decisions about how the sealift capability gap could and would be filled. The commissioning of the two Landing Helicopter Dock (LHDs) ships *Adelaide* and *Canberra* in 2014 and 2015 involved close examination of both lessons learned from East Timor and detailed assessment of likely future needs. These two ships will more than adequately fulfil the requirements of a future INTERFET-type of operation close to our shores. Furthermore, the new surface ship capability provided by the Air Warfare Destroyers (HMA Ships *Hobart*, *Brisbane* and *Sydney*) will enhance Australia's maritime surveillance capability and add to the RAN's strike and attack capability in a limited conflict. It is often said, and mostly cynically, that militaries are always preparing to fight the most recent war. In many respects, this is also true of the ADF. The recent past is often, if not usually, the best guide to the near future. There is, however, a plan to improve the information warfare and intelligence gathering side of the equation accompanying the delivery of explosive ordnance. Planning and preparing rightly focuses on clarifying the nature and as well as the potency of the threat in tandem with securing the most effective technology for ensuring national security is preserved and national interests are advanced.

The final but foremost lessons from East Timor relate to people. As ever, individual servicemen and servicewomen are the decisive factors in the conduct of warfare. Advanced equipment and superior tactics are irrelevant when people are untrained and ill-disciplined. Thankfully, the militias and their TNI supporters did not have any capacity to oppose INTERFET at sea. They had no vessels they could deploy and no anti-ship weapons of any consequence. They did not possess or use seaborne mines or attempt to damage ships at anchor with armed divers. Nevertheless, INTERFET's maritime assets needed to be employed to maximum operational effect and without making any situation ashore more fraught with unnecessary conflict or controversy. There were no accidents in Timorese waters despite the presence of so many warships and no-one lost their life at sea. INTERFET demonstrated that the 'people factor' remains a key strength of the ADF. The RAN was able to operate with the world's best navies and do so with confidence and competence. Further, the maritime element was well coordinated with the participating commending the Australians on the planning and execution of all operations. Australian naval personnel also demonstrated a flair for creativity, innovation and flexibility. In sum, INTERFET demonstrated that planning ability, sound training, fighting capability and practical success can only be achieved with good people.

While I remain far from convinced that all of the lessons from East Timor were learned and that all of INTERFET's legacies have been appreciated, it is clear that much of value can still be drawn from contemplating what went wrong and reflecting upon what went right in 1999. It does not matter whether insight or wisdom are acquired immediately after an event or perhaps two decades later, they are their own reward and worthy of pursuing.

CHAPTER 8

A military perspective

David Kilcullen

For many who served in East Timor during INTERFET, the enduring image of the campaign is of Australian soldiers as protectors and rescuers of the Timorese people. One iconic photograph shows a kneeling Australian soldier, rifle discretely slung behind him, taking the hand of a smiling local child while graffiti on the wall behind them proclaims: 'I LOVE YOU MILITARY INTERFEET [sic] FOREVER.'[1] This is how many INTERFET veterans would like to remember the mission, and certainly how the Australian Army would prefer that the nation remember it. But the Army also took away a parallel set of private institutional memories: lessons rarely discussed in public but ultimately more important today.

'I had been in Bosnia about three years earlier with the British, and by contrast Australia was a sad and badly prepared joke,' one officer told the author, Leigh Neville.

> The core failure was in our logistic support, but this was also compounded by lack of communications equipment, virtually no military police, and extremely lax control and discipline in [headquarters] at all levels. Timor was indeed a wake-up call, and we were extremely lucky that we did not face a serious opposition—the Taliban, or Iraqi insurgents ... would have carved us up.[2]

Though an immensely complex and multifarious large-scale operation like INTERFET is extraordinarily difficult to comprehend in the moment, let alone to recall later, at a distance of twenty years and multiple other conflicts, the aim of this chapter is to examine what the mission meant for the Australian Army as an institution. More particularly, the goal here is to explore a selection of lessons the Army learned from the operation, how these were applied in later campaigns, and their effect on the Army today.

The chapter will examine the conditions that shaped INTERFET, its principal impacts—for the Army's role in combined, joint, interagency operations; for manoeuvre operations in a littoral environment; for urban warfare and insurgency prevention, hardened, networked mobility and expeditionary logistics and sustainment—and its main outcome: a crucial wake-up call for what was soon to come in Iraq and Afghanistan.

Background conditions

Operational lessons are meaningless unless we first understand the background conditions under which those lessons were learned, as they existed during the campaign in question. Indeed, taking lessons out of context then misapplying them as a template for future operations is a recipe for disaster. Thus, context is critical. At the national level, three conditions shaped Australia's response to the crisis of 1999.

The first was a highly experienced National Security Committee of Cabinet, led by the Prime Minister, John Howard. This committee—the subset of Cabinet members, senior military and intelligence officers that handles matters of national security—sets the policy, planning parameters and public tone for any operation. In this case the Howard Government, in office since 1996, had become very experienced in managing national security through a series of events including small-scale peacekeeping in the Balkans, Middle East and elsewhere, the larger joint operation in Bougainville, the regional instability triggered by the Asian financial crisis in 1997 and the collapse of the Suharto Government in Indonesia in 1998. Ministers knew each other well, the Prime Minister had established an effective decision-making process, service chiefs and agency heads knew what was expected, and briefers were well-versed in how to gather and present the necessary information for decision-makers. This stood the country in good stead when the East Timor crisis erupted.

On the other hand, a second condition that shaped INTERFET was an extraordinarily strong inter-departmental reluctance to plan for combat.

Diplomats at the Department of Foreign Affairs and Trade (DFAT) feared that any appearance that Canberra might be planning a combat intervention would alarm Indonesia, embolden the East Timorese independence movement, encourage violence by both anti-independence militias and pro-independence guerrillas, undercut assurances of Australia's peaceful intent, and thus trigger the very crisis it was designed to deter.

For their part, Defence officials at Russell Offices and planners at theatre, division and brigade level within the Australian Defence Force (ADF) saw the immense risks (both for mission success and for the survivability of forces ultimately committed) of failing to plan for combat, launching an operation with insufficient time for intelligence and reconnaissance, or inadequate logistic preparation. They also believed that robust public planning and preparation would have a deterrent effect on the Indonesian military commanders who controlled the militias. In the event, this difference of opinion became an increasingly acrimonious interagency tussle. It meant that approval to plan was repeatedly delayed (though some unauthorised planning did take place) inter-departmental coordination was lacking at key points, and the operation—when, indeed, it went ahead—did suffer from limited intelligence.

As other participants recalled:

> Body armour had to be borrowed. The initial troops on the ground carried limited ammunition, with no immediate resupply available if the conflict had taken a sudden turn for the worse. There was also a lack of fresh rations, with many units eating field rations for the first eight weeks of the deployment. The lack of heavy-lift aircraft would lead directly to the later acquisition of a number of C-17 Globemasters. Tactical intelligence was poor; one participant told the author: 'Excellent strategic intelligence, and [this] was briefed. Crap tactical intelligence. We had no insight into [Indonesian] army disposition and AOs [areas of operation] and size of militia forces, and given that the TNI had been handing out guns like candy, whether or not there were any anti-armour weapons in play.'[3]

A final national-level condition for INTERFET was strong bipartisan public support for the mission. Circumstances in East Timor leading up to the independence referendum of August 1999 had been horrific, with lethal human rights abuses by government-backed militias and extensive property destruction and population displacement. After the referendum the violence escalated dramatically, hundreds of thousands of Timorese fled their homes and much of the province burned. For those on the political left, long concerned about Indonesia's human-rights record, intensive media coverage prompted calls for humanitarian intervention. For those on the right, many of whom had long been suspicious of Indonesia's regional role, and who felt a debt of honour toward the Timorese who had selflessly supported Australian guerrillas during the Second World War, the push for intervention was equally strong, making INTERFET one of the rare military operations with broad support across the spectrum. This meant that once the campaign commenced and planning shortfalls began to bite, the Government had the parliamentary and public backing to remedy them.

At the operational level, the most important condition was that the Army was operating at scale, in a warlike environment, for the first time since the 'Long Peace' began in 1973 with Australia's withdrawal from South Vietnam. This—along with the Defence of Australia (DOA) doctrine, which led to significant under-resourcing of the Army from the mid-1980s—partly explains Australia's lack of preparedness as noted earlier in comparison to the British Army, which had experienced no such long peace and had been continuously operating at scale in Northern Ireland, Germany, Iraq, Cyprus, the Balkans and elsewhere since the 1960s. In Australia's case, individual Army units—Engineers in Namibia and Cambodia, Infantry in Somalia, mixed forces in Bougainville—had deployed on multinational peacekeeping or peace enforcement missions, but INTERFET was the first time in the quarter-century since Vietnam that the Army had deployed multiple units and formations of all arms and services for an expeditionary operation in a combat environment, and it showed.

INTERFET was also the first time in recent memory that an Australian headquarters had commanded a multinational expeditionary force, serving as the framework nation into which other national contingents plugged, providing the backbone of command and control, communications, logistics and transportation for the overall force, and taking ultimate responsibility for the outcome.[4] Until this point—in Korea, Malaya, Borneo and Vietnam, and in both world wars—Australians had mostly served as one contingent among many, or under British or American control. Aside from allowing the Australian Army to rely on firepower, intelligence, transport and logistics from a senior partner, in all these campaigns Australians had been free to claim credit for our contribution to victory, while criticizing the senior partner's campaign direction and simultaneously avoiding the burden of responsibility for campaign failure. (Incidentally, INTERFET was also the last time this has happened—in Iraq and Afghanistan Australians served as contingents in a larger force under United States command, while Australian-led operations in the Solomon Islands and Bougainville or, indeed, in East Timor after INTERFET, have been peace operations.)

Mitigating the enormous challenges inherent in the role of lead nation in an expeditionary coalition was the fact that East Timor is reasonably close to home—the distance from Darwin to Dili is roughly seven hundred kilometres—enabling Australia to cope with the unaccustomed demand, though only barely at times. Likewise, the enemy never posed a direct threat to Australian territory, and Australia had no other significant military commitments at the time, other than the Peace Monitoring Group in Bougainville (which was not a combat operation), allowing the Army to focus on East Timor. As an infantry company commander deployed at the very outset of the operation, the author so frequently encountered old friends from across the Army and, in fact, the broader ADF, that it seemed as if the entire Army was in East Timor, and one wondered who was left at home to mind the shop. This prompted one key lesson of the campaign to which I will return: the need for a larger force.

At the tactical level, the environment was extraordinarily complex. It involved a mix of urban, jungle and mountainous terrain, wet-monsoon tropical conditions and often bad weather, in an underdeveloped territory with poor or non-existent roads, extremely limited connectivity and no ability to draw on local resources (which were either absent altogether or had been destroyed during the pre-deployment crisis). Littoral manoeuvre, including amphibious operations and the need to seize and then operate ports and airports, was a key part of the operation. The largest airmobile assault since Vietnam—and the largest ever conducted using solely Australian helicopters—went off without a hitch despite difficult flying conditions. Adding to the complexity of the mission were irregular and counter-guerrilla warfare against militias and their Indonesian military sponsors, security operations in remote frontier areas, long-range and long-duration jungle patrolling, armoured vehicle operations in jungle, urban and coastal zones, integration of special operations into conventional-force activity, public order tactics in destroyed or semi-destroyed urban areas, and humanitarian assistance for hundreds of thousands of displaced persons.

At the same time, once Indonesian regular forces left East Timor in the first weeks of the operation, INTERFET faced an enemy with very limited capability. As mentioned above, the militias lacked improvised explosive devices (IEDs)—the presence of booby-traps, mines or IEDs such as were later encountered in Iraq and Afghanistan would have complicated the operation. The enemy lacked artillery, mortars, or rockets, had no heavy machine guns or armoured vehicles, moved mostly on foot, possessed no maritime or air capability, had extremely limited radio-intercept and signals intelligence, and rarely operated in groups larger than a dozen or so. While they did possess advanced small arms, these were in small numbers and enemy weapons skills were poor to non-existent throughout the operation. Thus, while it is incorrect to suggest that INTERFET faced no enemy, the lack of enemy capability for significant combat (except during the first few weeks of the campaign) helped to ameliorate the challenge significantly.

Key lessons

With this context as background, the lessons that the Army took from Timor make more sense. The first, already mentioned, was the need for scale: the ability to operate at Brigade and perhaps Division level in a fully-resourced, self-reliant and nationally-supported manner. INTERFET highlighted the personnel-intensive nature of both peace enforcement and irregular warfare, while the operation's open-ended nature forced the Army to confront the need for multiple rotations into theatre. Army personnel numbers had been significantly cut during the Long Peace, and in Timor the service had to deploy such a large proportion of available forces, at such short notice, that other tasks were jeopardised, strategic reserves were stretched and specialised troops such as terminal operators, military police and petroleum engineers were fully committed. Critical assets such as the Army's S-70 Blackhawk helicopters and ASLAV armoured vehicles were also used at higher level of effort than anticipated, shortening their operational life and demanding additional maintenance and upgrades. Coming out of the operation, the Army successfully argued for an expansion in numbers, the creation of additional special forces, two new infantry battalions and associated support troops.

Expeditionary logistics and sustainment offered the second key lesson. During the DOA period since 1987, a series of defence efficiency reviews had stripped the Army of much of its expeditionary logistic capability, civilianising base tasks and logistic or maintenance functions, and replacing soldiers with contractors in key support roles. INTERFET showed that this process had gone too far, if the Army was expected to mount and sustain an expeditionary operation, even one so close to Australia. The ability to resupply food, water, ammunition and fuel faltered on several occasions during the operation while comfort items such as toiletries and reading materials were supplied by subscription from concerned citizens at home. As one datum point, having landed on the first day of the operation, the author ate his first hot combat-ration meal 10 days after deploying, and his first fresh meal in week 8 of the operation. Throughout INTERFET, troops slept under hootchies, in tents or in partially destroyed local dwellings, with air-conditioned accommodation a rarity. Thus, at times, heat exhaustion, dengue and malaria became threats to the mission.

As a consequence, after INTERFET the Army pushed (often unsuccessfully) for a greater ADF commitment to expeditionary logistics, maintenance, and transportation, and the 're-militarisation' of certain functions that had been civilianised during preceding defence reviews. At a deeper level, the major lesson was that the Army had been resourced for one strategic concept (DOA) while being employed—for many years—under another (de facto expeditionary) concept, operating as far afield as the Balkans and Africa while funded and resourced only for low-intensity conflict operations inside Australia, at the landward end of DOA's 'sea-air gap'.

The third lesson was that this sea-air gap was in fact a sea-air-land gap, with multiple islands and ground-based objectives that would need to be denied to an adversary, secured and held as bases for air and maritime operations, or seized to enable landward force projection within Australia's near north. It may seem strange that this lesson had to be re-learned in the very same area where the island-hopping campaign of 1942–45 had shown the requirement for agile land forces capable of amphibious and airborne operations to support air and naval forces in a joint campaign. But during DOA, expenditure on advanced air and naval assets and an expected 'strategic warning time' of ten years led policy-makers to prioritise the RAN and RAAF while counting on enough time to expand the Army if required. The experience of INTERFET suggested that even in a regional intervention scenario the Army would need capabilities for Joint Forcible Entry Operations—the seizing of airfields, ports and harbours against opposition, and rapidly putting them back into operation to facilitate follow-on air and naval operations—implying the need to conduct integrated multi-domain combat operations.

The Army's Future Land Warfare (FLW) analysts applied these insights in developing the concepts of 'Entry from Air and Sea' (EAS) and 'Manoeuvre Operations in the Littoral Environment' (MOLE) in the years immediately after INTERFET. While, to some extent, MOLE and EAS were overtaken by events in the War on Terrorism, their enduring influence can be seen in the Army's capabilities and concepts today. The Navy's acquisition of capable amphibious ships, prompted both by new operating concepts and shortage of sealift during INTERFET, also reflects this lesson, as does acquisition of C-17 Globemaster transport aircraft and upgrading of the C-130 fleet by the RAAF.

Urban operations were crucial to INTERFET's early stages, as the force landed at Komorro airfield then advanced overland in the face of military opposition to the port of Dili through a heavily damaged urban landscape in which many buildings were still burning. The force then confronted Indonesian regular troops at a petroleum loading terminal, in several urban checkpoints, and in the centre of Dili. Urban operations against militia included patrolling, large-scale sweeps and key point security. The manoeuvre phase lasted roughly four weeks, after which the mission settled into a steady state of security and counter-militia operations, also often in urban terrain. The Army was already aware of the need for improved urban operations training—the first units to deploy on INTERFET, from 3 Brigade, had conducted urban training in North Queensland months before the operation—but exercise facilities were generally small-scale, lacked instrumentation for advanced training, and did not simulate complex battalion—or brigade-sized urban operations. In the years after INTERFET, the Army invested in instrumented larger-scale urban facilities and focused on urban combat operations as well as low-intensity and security operations. These efforts paid off later in Iraq.

Another lesson that came into its own in Iraq and Afghanistan, but which had its origins in East Timor, was the need to enhance protected mobility and networked communications for the Army's combat forces significantly. As noted, the enemy in East Timor had no IED or mining capability and chose not to employ anti-armour weapons against the force. Even so, the M113 armoured personnel carriers (of Vietnam War vintage) and ASLAV light armoured vehicles deployed during INTERFET showed several inadequacies. The M113s showed their age, with frequent breakdowns, track breakages and equipment failures in the heavy terrain of East Timor, while off-road mobility for the wheeled ASLAVs was very limited, forcing them to keep close to roads and making their movements predictable. In part because of this predictability, one battalion-sized sweep with armoured vehicles conducted by 2 RAR late in 1999 in the Aidabaleten hinterland of East Timor's northwest failed to encounter a single enemy, and very few civilians, in an area known to be populated and with enemy presence. Radio systems (also ageing) broke down frequently, and tactical satellite (TacSat) communications terminals were rare below battalion level, hampering the force's ability to communicate— especially in urban, jungle and mountain terrain, which accounted for most of the operational area. The Army had already taken steps to develop a protected mobility vehicle (subsequently to become the Bushranger PMV) to enable mobility and communications for the motorised 6 Brigade, but this lesson—accelerated by experience in Iraq and Afghanistan in the years after INTERFET—resulted in the Army's 'Hardened and Networked Army' concept and a suite of subsequent equipment acquisitions that shaped today's force.

The need for improved integration between general-purpose and special operations forces (SOF) was another clear, though less often discussed, lesson from INTERFET. Early in the mission operations by the SOF Response Force (RESPFOR) proved effective in deterring Indonesian regular troops from committing atrocities in eastern East Timor, and disrupting militia activity in and around Dili. As the operation progressed, however, tensions developed between SOF and regular infantry battalions in Dili and in the border zone. These tensions were largely a result of compartmented planning which left battalions in the dark and not postured to support SOF activity within 'operations boxes' carved out of battalion areas of responsibility, sometimes without their knowledge. In several cases, RESPFOR monopolisation of scarce helicopter assets hampered conventional operations. On at least one occasion SOF operating on the edge of an operations box compromised the presence of a conventional reconnaissance patrol nearby, forcing its withdrawal.

The most intense combat engagement of the campaign—the Battle of Aidabasalala on 16 October 1999, fought when a six-man SASR patrol was compromised on insertion by approximately 60 militia—took place inside the 2 RAR area of responsibility, but the battalion was unaware of the patrol's presence and thus not postured to assist when it had to be extracted under fire, or to conduct a rapid follow-up to hunt down the militia involved, rendering the engagement indecisive. In subsequent operations, in Iraq but most particularly in Afghanistan, the Army learned from this experience and integrated SOF with designated general-purpose units into special operations task groups, while creating clearer lines of authority and territorial areas of operations. The success of SASR and Commandos in Afghanistan—operating across multiple conventional unit areas of responsibility—was a testament to the Army's improvement in this regard.

A final key lesson was the need for integrated media in the conduct of expeditionary operations. INTERFET was lucky to have a force commander in Major General Peter Cosgrove who instinctively understood the need to leverage relationships with the media in order to shape the operational environment. Key audiences included the Australian people, whose continuing support was vital to the operation, the governments of troop-contributing nations, who needed to be reassured that their contingents were being safely and appropriately employed and, not least, the enemy—including both the militia groups opposing INTERFET and their Indonesian military backers— who needed to be deterred, forced back from the border, and cowed through a series of integrated media and manoeuvre operations. This understanding of media operations was not necessarily widespread throughout the force, and in the aftermath of INTERFET media operations training was one key addition to the Army's training repertoire—one that stood the Army in good stead when the wars in Iraq and Afghanistan began.

Conclusion

INTERFET was a serious wake-up call. By imposing pressure on the Army that was severe enough to force significant adaptation, but not so severe as to destroy the force, the East Timor campaign arguably provided the impetus needed to stave off significant failures in subsequent, far more demanding, campaigns. It was a near-run thing, a testament to the Army's ability to improvise under pressure, and a timely warning of the need to improve certain key capabilities which turned out to be vital only a few years later when the 9/11 terrorist attacks plunged Australia into the War on Terrorism and led to substantial warfighting commitments in Iraq and Afghanistan. The lessons learned during INTERFET, and the process of adaptation that began in response to those lessons, helped generate significant growth in the size of the Army, including in combat troops, SOF, logistics and maintenance capabilities and certain specialised capabilities such as civil-military operations and improved tactical and strategic intelligence.

It led to the MOLE, EAS, Complex Warfighting and Hardened and Networked Army concepts that shaped the Army's force development and materiel acquisition in the decade after INTERFET, and prompted a renewed focus on counterinsurgency and counterterrorism, as well as improved efforts integrate general-purpose and special operations forces. The creation of Regular Army Commando units, already in the pipeline before INTERFET, received a boost from the experience of the campaign, while shortfalls in expeditionary logistics and sustainment helped prompt efforts (only partially successful) to revitalise key capabilities that had atrophied during the 'Long Peace' that followed the end of the Vietnam War.

It was also a warning to be humble, in seeking to predict the future strategic and operational environment in which the Army operates. A force designed for DOA was employed under very different circumstances and given radically different missions from those envisaged in the Continental Defence scenarios of the 1980s and 1990s. Likewise, vehicles such as the Bushranger (of which the author was a dedicated hater at the time, seeing them as useless for prospective operations) turned out to be extraordinarily successful years later in Afghanistan, saving many, many lives, again under radically different circumstances from those for which they were originally envisioned. As such the overall, most important lesson—as a generation of soldiers learned in East Timor—is that we will never be able to predict the future battlespace in sufficient detail to optimise for a single preferred scenario, and thus the Army needs to optimised for agility, versatility and adaptability in its own right. Today's Army in Motion and Multi-Domain Manoeuvre concepts, fundamental to how the Army sees itself today, two decades after INTERFET, are a direct result of this insight.

Endnotes

1   ABC News (Australia), *An INTERFET Australian soldier talking to a boy in East Timor*, file photo, at https://www.abc.net.au/news/2017–04-24/ an-INTERFET-australian-soldier-talking-to-a-boy-in/8467588

2   Neville, Leigh, *The Australian Army at War 1976–2016*, London: Bloomsbury, Kindle edition, locations 359–60.

3   *Ibid.* locations 344–49.

4   One apparent exception is the United Nations mission in Cambodia during 1992–95, a multinational mission commanded by Australian Major General John Sanderson, but this operation did not involve a formed Australian headquarters responsible for all aspects of operational support to the wider force, as in East Timor.

CHAPTER 9

An air perspective

Kym Osley

T he Royal Australian Air Force (RAAF) and air power contributed significantly to the success of the international intervention in East Timor in 1999. Much of the RAAF's involvement was 'behind the scenes'. While the RAAF air support was effective and its mission objectives were achieved, there were still many lessons learned by the RAAF and the air component of INTERFET. Some of the deficiencies identified as a consequence of the deployment have resulted in major changes to the contemporary Air Force. In this chapter I will explore the implications of INTERFET for the RAAF, particularly on air power sustainment and support, defence industry, force design, and command and control.

The RAAF commitment

At the strategic and higher operational levels, there was growing awareness that the RAAF might need to support an intervention force in East Timor.[1] The RAAF's initial contribution was part of *Operation Concord*. It included the air transport of police, military liaison officers and UN volunteers from RAAF Base Darwin to East Timor from June 1999 when UNAMET was deployed until INTERFET was established in mid-September.[2]

Following a series of security leaks early in 1999, there was increasing compartmentalisation of planning for possible operations in East Timor with many Air Force units not warned of their possible deployment until very near the time of deployment. During that month, several RAAF units were placed on higher readiness levels for *Operation Spitfire* and *Operation Warden*. Some 13 RAAF C-130 aircraft were re-located to RAAF bases at Darwin and Tindal late in August 1999 to support INTERFET operations.[3] The pre-positioning of F-111 strike-reconnaissance aircraft to RAAF Tindal took place from 28 August 1999, two days ahead of the independence ballot. At Tindal, they joined the F-18s of No 75 Squadron and also a large number of Army helicopters that could be used to insert selected Army units and Special Forces personnel.[4] On 6 September, less than a week after the independence ballot, the Australian Defence Force (ADF) initiated the *Operation Spitfire* contingency plan to evacuate UN and foreign nationals from East Timor with the descent into militia violence. During the next week, the RAAF and the Royal New Zealand Air Force (RNZAF) evacuated 2478 people from East Timor.

Two weeks later, INTERFET personnel embarked in seven Australian and New Zealand C-130s landed at Comoro Airfield on the edge of Dili. It was the morning of 20 September 1999. In addition to Army units, the aircraft also carried the lead element of No. 2 Airfield Defence Squadron and personnel from No. 381 Expeditionary Combat Support Squadron (ECSS). The four ECSS units that took part in these operations established an airhead at Comoro and managed more than 17,000 flights, 200,000 passengers and 3.2 million kilograms of cargo. Their exceptional performance was facilitated by RAAF personnel at Darwin, Tindal and Townsville, who overcame many obstacles to operate round-the-clock air movements, facilitate force preparation and provide general operational support. The RAAF C-130 fleet was quickly bolstered by transport planes from other air forces which combined to form the INTERFET Combined Air Wing (ICAW). Over five months, ICAW flew 1902 sorties and transported 26,600 passengers to and from East Timor. The RAAF also operated four Caribou aircraft from Baucau airfield, with a deployment to Comoro for four months to fly missions to remote inland areas.[5]

The United States contributed the *Tarawa* Class Landing Helicopter Amphibious (LHA) ship USS *Pelileu* which operated Cobra and Sea Stallion helicopters. Notably, the American ship was held in 'reserve'. She would only become directly involved in operations in the event of a marked escalation of hostilities in East Timor. Army helicopter operations continued throughout the INTERFET period. Important aerial photographic reconnaissance operations were conducted using fixed wing aircraft under the Army's overall direction. Maritime patrols were also conducted by five AP-3C Orion aircraft from No. 10 and 11 Squadrons. Photo reconnaissance and Pave Tack reconnaissance flights were conducted from 31 October 1999 by F/RF-111C aircraft from RAAF Tindal.[6] Despite media reports to the contrary, there were no documented interactions between INTERFET and Indonesian TNI aircraft over Timor in 1999.

INTERFET's legacies: force structure

After the withdrawal of Australian forces from South Vietnam in 1973, the RAAF had been structured for the defence of continental Australia based on a close strategic alliance with the United States. There was an expectation that the RAAF would, if the need arose, be adapted to support American or British led-Coalition operations further afield. In the late 1990s, the RAAF's force design had not taken account of the possibility that Australia would lead a coalition operation beyond the nation's contiguous waters without direct support from the United States or another well-equipped operational partner.[7] INTERFET changed strategic thinking. After 1999 it was clear that the ADF needed the ability to conduct independent regional operations in support of Australia's national interests.[8] The ability to project and support air power in a 'Timor-like' operation has become an accepted element in force design across the three services. For the RAAF, this changed thinking translated into maintaining a uniformed workforce of about 15 000 personnel and the procurement of many key 'enabler' capabilities that it previously relied upon the United States to provide. These capabilities included those provided by Boeing 737 Wedgetail Airborne Early Warning and Control (AEW&C) aircraft, the Airbus A330 KC-30A Multi-role Tanker Transport fleet and large strategic airlift assets such as the Boeing C17 Globemaster III.

The East Timor campaign also came at the end of a decade of successive force reductions. These reductions were prompted essentially by the need to reduce escalating costs at a time of increasing budget pressure.[9] The 1991 Force Structure Review (FSR) identified 4200 RAAF uniformed support positions of the total 22 000 in the Air Force to be shed over the remainder of the decade.[10] Only 2000 of these positions were to be offset through replacement with non-uniformed contractors.[11] Following the FSR, the

RAAF uniformed numbers were further trimmed through the 'Manpower Required in Uniform' process of the mid-1990s before being scrutinised by the 1996 Defence Efficiency Review (DER) and the subsequent Defence Reform Program (DRP) of 1997–98. The DRP proposed an overall reduction to 42,700 uniformed ADF personnel with an Air Force of about 8,000–10,000 uniformed personnel. The purpose of cutting the workforce was to 'fund improved capability'.

While the Air Force delivered acceptable levels of air power and air support during the operations in East Timor, this level of delivery was 'despite' rather than 'because of' recent reviews that had significantly eroded the workforce. INTERFET provided a timely 'real world' sense of what the Government expected from the ADF. The Chief of Air Force used the East Timor experience to argue against some of the more extreme Air Force workforce reduction proposals in retaining an Air Force of about 15,000 people.[12]

More broadly, the effectiveness of ADF operations in East Timor led the Government to consider more expansive use of the ADF and the RAAF in support of Australia's interests. Within four years of INTERFET and, for the first time in the 30 years since the end of the Vietnam Conflict, the RAAF was conducting air combat operations in the Middle East and deploying capabilities that were previously beyond the remit of planners.

Logistics and sustainment

Throughout the 1990s, a series of reforms and reviews of Defence reduced Air Force logistics-related personnel by 50 percent—from 4000 people to just 2000.[13] Not surprisingly, RAAF deployments in support of INTERFET highlighted limitations in critical logistics skill areas such as air terminal operators.[14] This was not the only area of deficiency.

The RAAF's Combat Support Group (CSG) was established shortly before East Timor. It was ideally suited to East Timor operations although it was ultimately short-staffed given the extended duration of the deployment.[15] The ability of CSG units to re-establish key airfield infrastructure and to staff the key air 'points of entry' to the country were critical to INTERFET's success. Since then the Air Force has invested considerably in expanding and extending CSG capabilities. It is now the largest group within the RAAF. During the past two decades it has demonstrated its ability to establish and support forward deployed operations around the world. To simplify planning, the Combat Support Coordination Centre (CSCC) was formed to coordinate all CSG expeditionary missions.[16] The CSCC's role is to take direction from Joint Operations Command and provide the CSG with mission-specific guidance. There are seven primary capabilities: expeditionary airbase support; fixed airbase support; evacuation handling centres; health support; security; airfield engineering; and communications.

The entire RAAF C-130 transport fleet were involved in the 'strategic' insertion and resupply of the unopposed INTERFET deployment. There were few additional airlift resources available for other contingencies during the INTERFET period.[17] Had the arrival of INTERFET been opposed, many more troops and a good deal more equipment would have been needed. The RAAF did not have this capacity. Since INTERFET, the RAAF has greatly expanded its strategic airlift logistics support capability with a large fleet of C-17 and KC-30A aircraft, supplemented with the C-130J and the C-27J battlefield air lifter.

The INTERFET experience also highlighted the inadequate involvement of logistics staff in the strategic planning process. The establishment and management of effective supply chains were impeded as a result. Partly in response to the INTERFET experience, a Joint Logistics Command (JLC) was established in 2000. The following year, the Chiefs of Staff Committee directed that logistic staff were to be fully engaged in future planning processes to ensure the requirements of combat support were fully met, and that the 'strategic J-4' function would be performed by the Commander, Joint Logistics. Additionally, the dedicated one-star position of Director GeneraL Logistics-Air Force was reinstated within Air Force Headquarters after being previously downgraded as a cost-cutting measure in the Defence Reform Program (DRP) of 1997–98.

Preparedness management

INTERFET involved almost every element of the operational Air Force for an extended period. It tested the preparedness limits of most areas of the RAAF.[18] The ability to crew RAAF assets supporting INTERFET, while maintaining even basic operational training at home bases, became increasingly problematic as the operation extended over many months.

Post-operation reports from INTERFET indicated that the deployment's short warning time considerably reduced the scope for workup training and for preparing equipment. The result was some units deploying with capability deficiencies.[19] This was compounded by some RAAF aircraft being 'fitted for but not with' some pieces of operational equipment. In simple terms, fiscal constraints in the 1990s had led to some aircraft being made compatible with key systems and weapons with the expectation that additional systems or weapons would be procured in the lead up to conflict. They were not.

The 2001 Preparedness Management Review was conducted with the lessons of INTERFET very much in mind. The consequence of the review was a much improved process for Defence (and the RAAF) to manage its preparedness levels. Since 2001, there has been an increased Air Force focus on maximising preparedness and optimising the training pipeline, work force planning, temporal discipline and the categorisation of its 'war fighters' to achieve a ready and sustainable capacity to meet higher command expectations.

The sustained focus on preparedness has produced results. The RAAF can now support Air Taskforces with multiple workforce rotations over extended periods. Furthermore, the concept of aircraft being 'fitted for but not with' specific equipment is no longer accepted. There is a general assumption that what the RAAF operates with on a day-to-day basis is the same capability that can be fielded in time of conflict. This insistence carries a training and equipment cost burden which has necessitated some tough choices for Defence in times of fiscal constraint over the past two decades years.

Timely data dissemination

The 1991 Gulf War introduced the term, 'data deluge', when the quantity of military information, data and intelligence far outstripped the capacity to disseminate the information in a timely manner. The ADF and RAAF relearned this lesson in 1999. The Australian military information technology capabilities fielded in support of INTERFET were unable to support the amount of information being generated by INTERFET forces.

The RAAF has since heavily invested in advanced Intelligence, Surveillance and Reconnaissance platforms, with suitable ICT bearers to transmit the data for timely Production, Exploitation and Dissemination. The investment in platforms is being matched with investment in the underlying ICT infrastructure through Defence programs such as Joint Project 2096 which aims to provide Air Force (and other) intelligence analysts with the ability to rapidly search and discover collected data to improve intelligence and decision support to the RAAF and the wider ADF.[20] The ability to share key information across the air battlespace, and to support decision making at all levels, is a key tenet of 'Plan Jericho'. The Jericho Team has been striving since 2014 to better connect the RAAF and to facilitate more efficient decision making.

Inclusive operational planning

INTERFET was the first time that the Australian military and the relevant government agencies had key responsibility for planning operations since Vietnam, more than 25 years before. It is perhaps not surprising that strategic planning processes needed to be redeveloped and there was a tendency for information and decisions to be embargoed.

The advent of the Air Operations Centre (AOC) embedded in Joint Operations Command has assisted in providing expert air power advice at the most senior levels, and in ensuring timely and appropriate dissemination of information to the tactical level to support effective execution of the operations. The operation of highly classified capabilities that now predominate in the RAAF means that most Squadrons routinely deal with Special Access Program information and key staff are cleared to much higher levels than was normal at the time of INTERFET. Also, the unique and specialist nature of many capabilities requires the early involvement of the staff from these tactical units in operational planning.

Coherent command and control in wartime and peacetime

The Australian Defence Force higher level command and control arrangements were still evolving in the years leading up to INTERFET.[21] The revised C2 arrangements for INTERFET were established after it became clear that an intervention would be required and Australia would lead it.[22] For the first time with INTERFET, Australia was designated both the commander of the coalition and responsible to the United Nations (UN), and an Australian national commander as well. COMAST managed 'national command' through a Commander, Australian Contingent and duly appointed Naval, Air and Logistic Component Commanders.[23]

The air C2 arrangements were complicated by both Air Force (and the subordinate Air Headquarters) and HQAST in some cases directing the activities of RAAF units. This was in part due to organisational complexities where there was not a single established Air Operations Centre supporting the designated Air Component Commander for INTERFET. In essence, Air Headquarters had an embedded air operations centre capability at its facility in Glenbrook. HQAST did not have a dedicated air operations cell. The *Operation Warden* and *Operation Spitfire* Air Component Commander was able to track some but not all air operations from his location in Darwin under Commander, INTERFET.

Following INTERFET, Defence further refined its approach to operational command and control. In 2003 a three-star officer, the Vice Chief of the Defence Force, was inserted into the operational chain at the strategic level. This initiative was followed in 2004 by the establishment of a Joint Operations Command (JOC) led by a dual-hatted VCDF. It was not until 2007 that Defence finally established a separate 3-star CJOPS.[24]

Air Force embedded an Air Operations Centre in Joint Operations Command at the initial stand-up of the Headquarters. The AOC operates under a Director General-Air who fulfils the role of Air Component Commander for ADF air operations where a dedicated Air Component Commander is not designated. The AOC concept is scalable, with modest staffing levels on a day-to-day basis, able to be rapidly increased through the use of trained personnel located in the various Force Element Groups and increasingly through the use of larger numbers of experienced Reservists. The RAAF continues to evolve the Air C2 and AOC concept. The ability to force assign air elements rapidly has been mastered and is demonstrated through recent operations such as OP RELEX, where maritime patrol force elements seamlessly transfer back and forth between Air Force and JOC as needed.

Defence Industry as a fundamental input to capability

The ADF and the RAAF had increasingly come to rely on the commercial support base in the lead up to INTERFET but many of the agreements and contracts were based on 'in garrison' support and were not expected to support an INTERFET-like scenario. Contractual arrangements where Defence paid a premium for industry to maintain flexible processes and the capacity to surge to support increased ADF activity when required were lacking.[25]

The lack of industry networks and standing arrangements geared to the logistic supply requirements of an operation the size and duration of INTERFET necessitated *ad hoc* establishment of ways of replenishing or compiling stockholdings at short notice, often without time to ensure best value for money. When mechanisms of procurement could not be immediately established, the consequences were delays in logistic supply. Compartmentalisation of information prior to the INTERFET deployment also meant that logisticians did not have the benefit of lead-time to put in place specific civil military arrangements for supply and movement of materiel for East Timor. This left them with a 'just in time' reliance on the availability of items from local vendors.

Since INTERFET, the RAAF has embraced the concept that Defence industry is a fundamental input to capability, and has established very effective arrangements with a number of businesses to support most of the 'in garrison' maintenance of its aircraft, to have the ability to ramp up support in times of operations, and to manage much of the technical and aircrew training required by the Air Force. The relationship has evolved over time to a close partnership where uniformed members are embedded in some contractor technical operations to maintain their technical mastery to better support deployed operations. Additionally, industry is increasingly supporting RAAF capabilities from earlier in the Capability Life Cycle, including working in partnership to deliver air projects and programs. This has maximised the availability of uniformed RAAF members for operations.

Conclusion

Lessons learned from INTERFET have clearly shaped, and continue to shape, the Air Force and its approach to the application of air power. Most critically, INTERFET re-set the level of capability and capacity expected of the RAAF after a decade of cost-cutting reviews and workforce reductions. It resulted in Air C2 being integrated into the Joint C2 arrangements that have subsequently served both the RAAF and the ADF well. The RAAF has built an impressive air operations support capability within its Combat Support

Group over the past 20 years, and has leveraged Defence industry support where it has been effective to do so. The RAAF is no longer reliant on the United States for key enablers, such as ISR, AEW&C, air refuelling and heavy airlift, and has demonstrated the ability to deploy independently and sustain a balanced and very capable Air Task Group in recent operations. How many of these changes would have happened without the INTERFET deployment is difficult to determine. At some point the need for these initiatives and innovations would have become apparent. The events of 1999 increased their urgency, demonstrating why change was needed and the practical benefits that would flow to the Air Force and to the entire ADF as a consequence of better coordination, different equipment and retained corporate expertise.

Endnotes

1   A Chief of the Defence Force (CDF) Warning Order issued in Defence on 5 February 1999 stated the possibility that the ADF 'may become involved in either multilateral or a limited range of unilateral operations, such as evacuations.' It was assessed that peace-keeping operations in East Timor 'may be conducted in a high risk environment resulting in ADF casualties' and that they had potential to be protracted. The ADF was to be prepared if Australia was approached to take the lead in a multilateral operation. https://www.anao.gov.au/sites/g/files/net616/f/anao_report_2001-2002_38.pdf. On 11 May 1999, Defence began planning for Operation Spitfire, the possible involvement of the ADF in an evacuation of UN, Australian and certain other nationals from East Timor. The Minister for Defence, John Moore, announced on 11 March 1999 that a second brigade based in Darwin would be brought to 28 days operational readiness.

2   Accessed at http://airpower.airforce.gov.au/APDC/media/PDF-Files/Doctrine/AAP1000-H-The-Australian-Experience-of-Air-Power-1st-Edition.pdf on 29 August 2019, pp148-150.

3   https://www.aph.gov.au/About_Parliament/Parliamentary_Departments/Parliamentary_Library/Publications_Archive/CIB/cib9900/2000CIB03 accessed on 17 Aug 19

4   The Australian Army had up to 33 specially equipped long-range Blackhawk helicopters as well as an assortment of Iroquois (4) and Kiowa (8) helicopters.

5   Accessed on 7 September 2019 at http://airpower.airforce.gov.au/APDC/media/PDF-Files/Doctrine/AAP1000-H-The-Australian-Experience-of-Air-Power-1st-Edition.pdf on 29 August 2019. Pp148-150.

6   These reconnaissance flights were conducted with Indonesian diplomatic approval and started on 31 October 1999 following the withdrawal of the TNI. These missions continued until 9 December 1999.

7   Strategic guidance at the time, laid down by the Government in 1997 in Australia's Strategic Policy (ASP 97), required the ADF to develop capabilities to defeat attacks against Australia, and to provide substantial capabilities to defend Australia's regional strategic interests. In terms of the Government's priorities for operational interoperability with other countries, ASP 97 gave highest priorities to the United States, then New Zealand, then the countries comprising the Association of South East Asian Nations (ASEAN). Little reason was seen to invest in interoperability with countries beyond Southeast Asia.

8   https://www.victoria.ac.nz/strategic-studies/documents/strategic-briefing-papers/east-timor.pdf accessed on 17 August 2019. East Timor represented a new scenario for Australian strategic planning for the future with Australia taking the lead in organising a coalition of the willing to respond to crises. https://www.anao.gov.au/sites/g/files/net616/f/anao_report_2001-2002_38.pdf accessed on 18 August 2019.

9   http://www.defence.gov.au/SPI/publications/ForceStructureReview1991_opt.pdf accessed on 7 September 2019.

10   The planned strength of the ADF for 30 June 1987 was Navy 15,732, Army 32,000 and Air Force 22,797; a total strength of 70,529. The reduction from a peak in 1981-82 (75,000) reflects the Government's decisions on the aircraft carrier and naval fixed-wing aviation, and a reduction of 677 in the authorised terminal strength of the Army in the 1985-86 Budget. http://www.defence.gov.au/Publications/wpaper1987.pdf accessed on 7 September 2019.

11   http://www.defence.gov.au/SPI/publications/ForceStructureReview1991_opt.pdf accessed on 6 September 2019. See Table 1 on page 27.

12   For example, in 1998 at the time of DRP, the CAF was asked to consider options for the RAAF that had only 4000 people in uniform. Under this construct, only the aircrew and a few technical and operations support staff would be uniformed, and the remainder civilianised.

13   https://www.anao.gov.au/sites/g/files/net616/f/anao_report_2001-2002_38.pdf. Source: Compiled by the ANAO from information supplied by Defence.

14   https://www.anao.gov.au/sites/g/files/net616/f/anao_report_2001-2002_38.pdf

15   17 May 2018 was the twentieth anniversary of CSG. https://www.govhouse.qld.gov.au/the-governor-of-queensland/speeches/2018/may/20th-anniversary-of-raaf-combat-support-group.aspx

16   https://www.airforce.gov.au/about-us/structure/air-command-headquarters/combat-support-group

17   https://www.aph.gov.au/About_Parliament/Parliamentary_Departments/Parliamentary_Library/Publications_Archive/CIB/cib9900/2000CIB03

18   For example, almost the entire F/RF-111C aircrew workforce was needed to provide a 24/7 alert response from RAAF Tindal. In some cases, the exchange officers that occupied key positions within RAAF operational flying units were not

authorised to participate by their parent nations and necessitated other RAAF air crew members at lower preparedness levels to take their place.

19   https://www.anao.gov.au/sites/g/files/net616/f/anao_report_2001-2002_38.pdf

20   JP 2096 is a multi-phase programme that aims to enable intelligence analysts to rapidly search and discover collected data to improve intelligence and decision support to then Australian Defence Force.

21   *Exercise Kangaroo 1995* revealed deficiencies in coordination between the various operational headquarters. In 1996, a permanent 2-star Commander Australian Theatre (COMAST) was established under VCDF supported by HQAST and a joint intelligence centre. From July 1999, VCDF was no longer responsible for the oversight of operations, with a 2-star officer (COMAST) performing this role. This resulted in a situation where the 2-star COMAST dealt with same-ranked environmental commanders in the respective. Serviceshttp://www.defence.gov.au/ADC/publications/documents/joint_studies/JSPS_1_Australias_Joint_Approach.pdf

22   These C2 arrangements were unique in Australia's experience and reflected the complex requirements of a large international coalition force on a mission to restore peace through an offshore deployment. The arrangements had to protect the national interests of troop contributing countries, including those of Australia as the lead nation, contribute to military effectiveness and efficiency, and have regard to UN requirements. The C2 arrangements put in place for INTERFET involved a complex force assignment and command process whereby Australian forces were assigned by the CDF to COMAST, then to COMASC for national command and COMINTERFET for operational command. At the same time COMINTERFET was assigned forces from other troop contributing nations and was given other responsibilities such as coalition integration and reporting to the Australian Government and the United Nations.

23   HQINTERFET Post Operations Report, 23 Feb 2000 para. 106.

24   http://www.defence.gov.au/ADC/publications/documents/joint_studies/JSPS_1_Australias_Joint_Approach.pdf accessed on 7 September 2019.

25   https://www.anao.gov.au/sites/g/files/net616/f/anao_report_2001-2002_38.pdf accessed on 7 September 2019

CHAPTER 10

Whole-of-government thinking

Alan Ryan

T he International Force East Timor (INTERFET) operation in 1999–2000 represented a critical point in the evolution of civil-military-police coordination for Australian government offshore deployments.[1] The previous quarter century had seen few offshore operations, none on this scale, and certainly none where Australia was called upon to play a leadership role. Australian government departments and agencies were not practiced in delivering coordinated national and coalition operations. Government strategic policy and military doctrine precluded the consideration of, and planning for, 'expeditionary operations', and both military and civilian capability to do so was extremely limited.[2] So the experience of deploying at extremely short notice, to undertake an operation that only one year earlier was unthinkable, holds lessons for future unanticipated 'black swan' interventions.

The subsequent experience of coordinating national operations in Afghanistan, Iraq and the Solomon Islands benefited from this experience. The fact that they were sometimes of higher intensity and more protracted should not detract from the fact that INTERFET represented an extremely high-risk operation. Australia's vital interests were engaged and the deployed occurred within 500 nautical miles of our coastline.

In short, since INTERFET, the Australian Government has recognised the importance of multiagency preparedness. It has learned that personalities are more important than process and that, consequently, governments and agencies need to invest effort in building robust and positive interagency relationships. Whole-of-government participation in exercises, joint education and training, cross-agency postings, and liaison arrangements are now common. Perhaps more important is the message that success is no longer the province of single agencies acting to the detriment of a whole-of-government approach. The Government expects that Commonwealth departments and agencies will work together seamlessly. It is incumbent on civilians, military and police to pursue that objective. As Prime Minister Morrison stressed in his August 2019 address to the Australian Public Service (APS):

> where disruption and cultural change are needed is in breaking down the bureaucratic silos and hierarchies that constrain our capacity to fix problems ... We need an APS that's more joined-up internally and flexible in responding to challenges and opportunities.[3]

A watershed for Australia's crisis management culture

Australia's commitment to the International Force East Timor (INTERFET) marks a watershed in the maturing of Australia's commitment to what we now know as the 'Integrated Approach' to crisis management. At the time, however, it was anything but integrated. For those factors within Australia's control (and many factors were not), two characteristics stand out. First, that the existence of the National Security Committee of Cabinet created a level of strategic cohesion that would otherwise have been lacking. Second, that it was the operational performance of the force that deployed and the extraordinary efforts of relatively junior civilian officials and police, operating often in isolation, that delivered results on the ground. Twenty years later, the lessons of the INTERFET deployment have been reinforced by the lessons of subsequent operations. Australian government agencies, working together on operations, need at least three things: alignment at the strategic level; coordination in operational planning; and, cooperation among the deployed multiagency partners.[4]

The popular memory of the Australian involvement in INTERFET is of a successful intervention and perhaps reflects relief that Australia's relationship with Indonesia was not damaged in the long-term by those events. Within government, operations after the September 2001 terrorist attacks in the United States quickly refocused strategic policymakers' and operational planners' attention. For those who have never worked in government it is difficult to describe the fog and friction that accompanies everyday events, much less the management of fast-moving crises. It is all too easy to criticise at a comfortable distance how government agencies respond in a crisis.

This chapter does not do that. A relatively new Government and an array of government departments and agencies were forced to contend with a crisis over which they had limited influence. On the whole they performed better than could have been expected. But the crisis management framework in government; the cross-agency coordination architecture; and, many organisations and individuals were poorly prepared for the challenges which they faced. The East Timor crisis of 1999 remains important as it forced Australia to move from an essentially siloed departmental approach to adopt an integrated approach to crisis management. This chapter briefly describes some of those lessons.

The first lesson is how the Howard Government's newly introduced National Security Committee of Cabinet (NSC) provided an important political focus for decision-making. At the same time, the other standing senior committees of government were optimised for the routine conduct of government business, not to manage a unique and unanticipated situation. Faced with circumstances outside the conventional frame of reference, many officials reacted with what the Secretary of Defence, Dr Allan Hawke, identified in February 2000 as 'learned helplessness'.[5]

Second, the crisis forced the creation of a taskforce arrangement to do the untidy but necessary job of interagency coordination that existing committee processes and internal departmental taskforces could not do. Crisis response requires bespoke, adaptive interagency tasks forces to communicate, coordinate, cajole and 'grease the wheels' of government.

Third, where any one government has limited capacity to influence the course of events, relationships are important. Australia was a significant participant in events, but it was only one of many players. As it transpired, diplomatic and personal relationships with other country's nationals, international organisations (IOs), non-government organisations (NGOs), diaspora groups and private sector entities were critical in resolving a situation that went very bad, very quickly.

Finally, for contemporary crisis management, preparation is everything. Government departments and agencies need to see themselves as part of a complete solution, able to collaborate to achieve national policy and operational outcomes. This integrated approach will not occur by default. Organisations and individuals need to be sufficiently professional to form multiagency teams at no notice to work towards politically directed strategic objectives. This necessity requires the formation of diverse teams comprised of deep subject matter experts from a variety of professions, organisations and disciplines who can work together. To be able to collaborate without notice, they must have experienced common education and training. Importantly, they need to have exercised together, so that the first time they meet to solve problems is not in the middle of a crisis. Individually, they need to have acquired the resilience to work across cultural boundaries in stressful and confronting circumstances.

Hope is not a method: the need for flexible processes to facilitate crisis decision-making

The historical record reflects the fact that we still have some way to go to a final and balanced assessment of the performance of government departments and agencies in a crisis. And the situation in East Timor was a crisis. Events unfolded swiftly in 1999, turning a 24-year old policy position on its head as Australia came to terms with the fact that, no matter what Australia said, East Timor might separate from Indonesia and become an independent state.

There is a tendency to consider INTERFET in isolation as it was the moment in which Australia stepped up to lead the coalition. But to do so is a mistake. INTERFET was part of a continuum of events. Australians played a considerable part in diplomacy, policy and operations before and after the INTERFET deployment. As Major General Michael Smith, the Director General East Timor in Defence during 1999 and subsequently Deputy Force Commander in the United Nations Transitional Administration in East Timor (UNTAET), explained:

> INTERFET should not be seen as a single operation, but as part of a UN trilogy of missions—UNAMET, INTERFET and UNTAET—in which Australia played a major role. These three missions and INTERFET

in particular, highlighted a number of key strategic lessons that have continuing relevance to Australia's security.[6]

An issue of the *Australian Journal of International Affairs* published in the immediate aftermath of INTERFET contained scathing assessments by some of Australia's most highly respected and competent strategic analysts. In particular, Professor William Maley, subsequently Professor of Diplomacy at the Australian National University's Asia-Pacific College of Diplomacy, criticised the way that some influential policy-makers clung to the policy position that Australia should support Indonesia's assertion of sovereignty over East Timor regardless of the consequences. Maley suggested that there had been a bureaucratic culture in the Department of Foreign Affairs and Trade (DFAT) that 'systematically discourages critics of certain orthodoxies and encourages conformity rather than imagination'.[7] Maley claimed that in the run-up to this crisis there was:

a tendency in DFAT to muddle through and hope for the best, rather than to engage in proper contingency planning. Such disjointed incrementalism has its virtues when one is dealing with low-risk or routine matters but it is likely to be disastrous as a means of dealing with an imminent or actual crisis ... many staff in a range of federal government departments who should have been involved in high-level planning for the crisis which eventuated were otherwise occupied at the time when planning should have been at its height.[8]

This assessment was reiterated in David Connery's 2010 scholarly analysis *Crisis Policymaking: Australia and the East Timor Crisis of 1999*.[9] Connery went further and identified a tendency for DFAT to engage in 'best case' thinking while Defence commenced consideration of 'worst case' scenarios.

I must admit to not being an objective observer in this debate. During 1999–2000 at the direction of the then Chief of the Defence Force, Admiral Chris Barrie, I was engaged in collating lessons learned from the conduct of the operation. Like any other young player, I was fully immersed in the partisan nature of inter-agency politics. With the advantage of distance it is clear that for the most part the departmental cultures were doing precisely what they were designed to do, but no provision had been made to reconcile those different perspectives under pressure.

It is not surprising that DFAT staff sought to preserve the peace at all costs. The outcome of an international intervention was unclear and we expect our diplomats to seek negotiated, rather than military, solutions where possible. Equally, it was important that Defence planners were able to investigate operational options without committing themselves to action. Military preparedness is founded on rigorous planning for all possible contingencies.

Other departments and agencies also had a stake in their voices being heard, particularly when it became obvious that their staff were to be deployed offshore. Then, and even more now, government officers had responsibilities and even liability for the safety and security of their deployed staff. With respect to the policy guidance provided Australian government agencies could have improved their performance and readiness by cooperating to produce earlier, bolder, whole-of-government assessments of the unfolding situation.

In 1999 it was understandable that the interagency crisis management framework reflected the deliberate, siloed arrangements that had prevailed in the final phases of the Cold War and the hopeful 'End of History' period that followed. Twenty years of persistent conflict has put paid to that approach. My colleagues at the United Kingdom's Stabilisation Unit summed up the current state of their thinking about how to achieve joined-up coordination in a 2010 paper:

> When asked to work together government departments generally look to liaise or coordinate, to retain their own teams whilst negotiating with other departments. Experience from the field has shown in the complex, fast moving and highly pressurised environment of conflict this does not work. The transactional costs are too high.[10]

We now know that crisis response requires the addition of simple, widely understood coordinating mechanisms to supplement the machinery of government. The events of 1999 drove the adoption of bespoke arrangements to meet the demands of the extraordinary circumstances of the day. Two decades on, there is no going back to rigid, process-driven structures in a digitised era of more closely integrated government. Form must follow function. A more professional whole-of-government workforce must be able to work smoothly and rapidly across portfolio boundaries. Defence Joint doctrine will recognize this soon, by formally adopting the Integrated

Approach in the forthcoming edition of its capstone publication, *War and Conflict*. It will suggest that in a complex crisis government should give consideration to applying the:

> *Integrated Approach*: A method of strategic planning and operational execution where all government agencies coordinating a task establish a single multi-disciplinary and multi-departmental team to design, plan and conduct an operation.

What worked, and what did not

Two excellent studies by David Connery and by the RAND Corporation (commissioned by the Australian Civil-Military Centre) chart the progress of crisis policy-making in 1999. There is no need to restate their findings here.[11] Clearly, the creation of the National Security Committee of Cabinet (NSC) in 1996 provided an essential executive level of government forum for critical political decision-making and ensuring that the responsible ministers and most senior officials could have their say.[12] The NSC is a unique Cabinet committee in that the Chief of the Defence Force and Secretaries for each public service department represented by a Minister on the NSC attend meetings in an advisory capacity. The deliberations of the NSC are naturally conducted at the strategic level. The time available does not permit the NSC to consider the detail of deployments. Other bodies exist to do just that. In 1999 it demonstrated its value as the executive decision-making forum for issues of vital national interest.

Notably, as early as April 1999 a new interdepartmental committee led by Bill Paterson, an assistant secretary in the Department of the Prime Minister and Cabinet (PM&C), was formed to discuss 'options and implications' arising from the situation. Comprised of APS Band One level representatives from DFAT, ONA, AusAID, Defence, the Australian Federal Police and the Australian Electoral Commission, the committee played an important information-sharing role at the all-important working level. It was, however, a process-driven committee. It did not have the remit or the capacity to consider military operations, much less commence contingency planning for whole-of-government operations.[13] The important point for this discussion was recognition that PM&C, which did not possess a policy lead on any single issue under consideration, had an important coordinating role in what became a whole-of-government effort. The committee, which met fortnightly, had its limitations. It was not a standing interagency policy task force. Throughout the prelude to the Australian-led intervention, policy was made within departments that were dispersed across Canberra. It was not made by officers and officials who were co-located in the same offices or buildings and able to consult with each other immediately or easily.

There has been more recent acknowledged that PM&C can play a very useful role establishing inter-agency policy task forces. Ric Smith, formerly Secretary of the Department of Defence and Australia's Special Envoy for Afghanistan and Pakistan, produced a report on the lessons to be learned from Australia's whole-of-government mission in Afghanistan that recommended:

> All relevant departments and agencies should be involved in whole-of-government policy development and planning from the outset of any proposed cross-border intervention. This approach is premised in the reality that all military actions have policy consequences, and thus an offshore deployment of the ADF should be seen as a matter that engages a full range of Australia's international policy interests.[14]

As it turned out a more coherent inter-agency task force was established to coordinate national policy and to report on policy development to the NSC. Led by the Director-General of the Australian Secret Intelligence Service (ASIS), Allan Taylor, the Taylor Committee comprised a standing secretariat of executive level staff drawn from DFAT, Defence, Immigration, AusAID and PMC and more senior officials who met daily. Connery concluded: 'the decision to establish the Taylor Committee reflected the Prime Minister's desire to streamline policy advice and a level of concern about inter-departmental coordination'.[15] Regrettably, the secretariat did not assemble until 21 September which was the day after INTERFET began to deploy. The full committee did not meet until 27 September.

As the crisis gained momentum, departments and agencies exceeded their usual workloads in providing expert advice. The work involved in developing policy options for Cabinet consideration required considerable effort at branch and desk officer level. Policy advice is thrashed out at the working level by relatively junior executive-level staff who are the responsible desk officers and their senior executive managers. Within DFAT, the East Timor Crisis Centre provided policy guidance, including regular briefings and background information to inform the negotiations leading to the formation of the coalition. Within the Department of Defence an East Timor Policy Unit was established on 7 September. It would support the Minister and Defence Executive; provide political-military guidance; and, coordinate the work of the Strategic Policy and International Policy Divisions. The practical task of managing the offers of coalition contributions was the task of INTERFET Branch which was established in Strategic Command Division within Australian Defence Force Headquarters. These Band One/One Star led units were in constant communication. They were not co-located nor did they possess a common leadership. Although able to cooperate, they were too physically discrete to collaborate at the level required to achieve an integrated approach.[16]

The Taylor Committee remains an important innovation because, prior to its establishment, it was expected that the existing committee hierarchy was sufficient to manage the routine business of government. But that is very much the point. Confronted with unique and rapidly changing circumstances, there is always a requirement to create shortcuts to expedite decision-making. A hierarchy consisting of the NSC; the Secretaries Committee on National Security (SCNS); the then Strategic Policy Coordination Group (SPCG); various inter-departmental Emergency Task Forces (IDETFs—a misnomer, because they are not task forces, they are committees); and interdepartmental committees (IDCs) proved too bureaucratic for an unfamiliar crisis. Such bodies are largely deliberative and facilitate the sharing of information. They do not generally make decisions, and in a rapidly developing crisis they are too slow to formulate advice for the executive branch of Government, principally ministers.

Since 1999 it has become clear that tailor-made crisis taskforces are needed to provide a 'joined-up' perspective, which might not actually represent a consensus view. Nonetheless, they can cut through departmental differences and, at the very least, provide an alternative way forward. It is also important as a 'fail-safe' measure to ensure that important matters are not forgotten because departments assume that others have the policy lead. It is all too easy in a crisis to focus on one's own immediate responsibilities and tasks and to neglect the interdependencies between actors or simply fail to see the bigger picture.

Influence in the absence of authority

There is a tendency among some commentators external to government to ascribe to government more control over a crisis than could ever be the case. This was very definitely so in 1999. Once the force had deployed, INTERFET was able to establish conditions of security on the ground. Given the limited points of entry, complex terrain, confused situation and sensitivities in dealing with Indonesian authorities, this naturally took some time. Twenty-two countries contributed military forces to the coalition, many of whom had never even trained together.[17] Over the UNAMET-INTERFET-UNTAET period from 1999–2002, various UN agencies, police, government aid and donor providers, non-government organisations and private sector groups were active in East Timor. Local systems of governance did not cease to be of relevance and the local political factions, FRETILIN and FALANTIL, were very much a part of the scene. Religious groups, notably the Catholic Church, were also important providers of practical and pastoral services.

The lesson for subsequent operations is that interventions on this scale are not merely complicated, they are complex. By making this distinction, I mean that no military or police commander, or civilian official, has very much practical power or real authority over all the participants in a disrupted society. Coalition contributors are quick to play the red card and so the mission leadership leads by exerting influence, not by imposing directive authority. At the time, General Cosgrove attracted much just praise for his leadership style which was ideally suited to the circumstances. He was not alone in adopting a measured approach. A heavy hand from any of those involved would not have worked.[18] A key lesson for subsequent operations is that adaptive modes of leadership are required by leaders at every level. This sort of leadership needs to be taught. Civilians, military and police must know how to lead across boundaries, operate in unfamiliar cultural contexts, develop their intent centrally, plan cooperatively and radically delegate execution. They require a well-developed understanding before an operation of the capabilities, operational cultures, and capacity to engage of all the actors that they will encounter.[19] Before INTERFET this was not a part of our whole-of-government culture. Since then it has become embedded in our way of doing things as we seek to create an ever more integrated national crisis management framework synchronised at every level—not just in NSC. To do that we have learnt the necessity of investing in preparedness.[20]

A closing reflection

My closing point is this: all of government, not just the ADF, must invest in preparedness. The 2008 Senate Standing Committee Inquiry into Australian involvement in peacekeeping operations was established to learn the lessons from operations, including INTERFET, to assist government prepare for future operations. The Committee found that:

> if Australia is to achieve an effective whole-of-government training framework, it must begin by finding a way to integrate the separate training programs and ad hoc courses into a coherent whole. While allowing agencies to continue to train their personnel for their specific functions, this whole-of-government approach would avoid duplication, identify and rectify gaps in training and promote better cooperation and coordination among all participants in the field. A central agency is required to provide overarching strategic guidance and planning that would give coherence to the agencies' individual and joint education and training programs.[21]

The Australian Civil-Military Centre was established in response to the Senate committee's recommendation. I have been proud to lead the agency for a number of years. We do not seek to control the work of departments or other government entities. Our mandate is to add value to whole-of-government activity. For me and my colleagues, coordination involves sharing information, identifying best practice, building networks, establishing partnerships and providing the institutional memory for whole-of-government initiatives that have worked and also for those that have struggled.

As a consequence of the East Timor experience, we know that ensuring strategic alignment of national objectives, providing for operational coordination acmong contributing organisations and setting expectations for collaboration in the field needs to happen well before a crisis begins. As INTERFET showed, we no longer have the luxury of a long pre-deployment phase in which to plan and prepare. We go with what we have. It is therefore incumbent on all departments and agencies to prepare their people for future strategic shocks and unexpected operational demands. The continuing need is for leaders who have attended whole-of-government education and training programs, such as those provided by the National Security College and the Australian Civil-Military Centre; coordinators who have participated in challenging multi-agency exercises that prepare them for activities that challenge institutionalised customs and conventions; administrative staff who have gained experience outside their home agencies by being prepared to work elsewhere, including in private sector roles and non-government organisations; and, imaginative thinkers who have served as liaison officers in different portfolios and who are fully prepared for these critical roles ahead of taking up their jobs.

The 1999 crisis marked the end of the long torpor from which Australia's operational culture had entered following the withdrawal of Australian forces from South Vietnam in 1973. In terms of civil-military-police preparedness, it is essential that we do not forget the many lessons that can be learned from a period of uncertainty and instability which challenged Australian national government and its processes.

Endnotes

1   John Gordon and Jason Campbell, *Organising for Peace Operations; Lessons Learned from Bougainville, East Timor and the Solomon Islands*, RAND Corporation 2016, p. 37.

2   N Jans, S Mugford, J Cullens, J Frazer-Jans, *The Chiefs: A Study of Strategic Leadership*, Commonwealth of Australia, 2013, pp. 69–70.

3   Prime Minister Scott Morrison, *Speech to the Institute of Public Administration*, 19 Aug 2019, Parliament House, Canberra, <<https://www.pm.gov.au/media/speech-institute-public-administration>> accessed 12 September 2019.

4   John Gordon and Jason Campbell, *Organising for Peace Operations: Lessons Learned from Bougainville.*; Stabilisation Unit, *The Integrated Approach is essential*, <http://www.sclr.stabilisationunit.gov.uk/top-ten-reads/comprehensive-integrated-approach/36-the-integrated-approach-is-essential> accessed 31 January 2018.

5   A Hawke, 'Address to the National Press Club', 17 February, 2000, p. 2, <<http://www.defense-aerospace.com/articles-view/verbatim/4/16254/what%27s-the-matter-with-australian-mod.html>> accessed 12 September 2019.

6   Michael Smith, 'INTERFET and the United Nations', chapter 1 in J Blaxland (ed.) *East Timor Intervention: A Retrospective on INTERFET*, Melbourne University Press, 2015. p. 25.

7   William Maley, 'Australia and the East Timor Crisis: Some Critical Comments', *Australian Journal of International Affairs*, Vol 54, No. 2, 2000, pp. 151–161, p. 159 quoted.

8   Maley, 'Australia and the East Timor Crisis: Some Critical Comments', p. 159.

9   D Connery, *Crisis Policymaking: Australia and the East Timor Crisis of 1999*, ANU E-Press, 2010, see pp. 23–28, 56–68.

10   UK Stabilisation Unit, *Responding to Stabilisation challenges in hostile and insecure environments: Lessons Identified by the UK Stabilisation Unit*, November 2010, p. 9. <<https://issat.dcaf.ch/download/2669/23086/UK%20SIN%20Top%20Lessons%20from%20Stabilisation%20and%20Conflict.pdf >> accessed 12 November 2019.

11   Connery, *Crisis Policymaking*; Gordon and Campbell, *Organising for Peace Operations.*

12   Connery, *Crisis Policymaking*, pp. 6–9.

13   Gordon and Campbell, *Organising for Peace Operations*, pp. 40–41,

14   Australian Civil-Military Centre, *Afghanistan: Lessons from Australia's Whole-of-Government Mission*, Commonwealth of Australia, 2016, p. 19.

15   Connery, *Crisis Policymaking*, p. 39.

16   Alan Ryan, *Primary Responsibilities and Primary Risks: Australian Defence Force Participation in the International Force East Timor*, Study Paper 304, Land Warfare Studies Centre, Canberra, 2000, pp. 38–9.

17   Alan Ryan, 'The Strong Lead-nation Model in an ad hoc Coalition of the Willing:
     Operation Stabilise in East Timor', *International Peacekeeping*, vol. 9, no. 1, Spring
     2002, pp. 23–44.

18   Peter Cosgrove, 'Commanding INTERFET', in Blaxland (ed.) *East Timor
     Intervention*, pp. 108–11; Ryan, *Primary Responsibilities and Primary Risks*,
     pp. 71–2.

19   Excellent recent discussions of this requirement include: J Mattis with B West,
     Call Sign Chaos: Learning to Lead, Random House, New York 2019, pp. 240–1;
     S McChrystal, *Team of Teams: new rules of engagement for a complex world*,
     Penguin, New York, 2015; D Williams, *Leadership for a Fractured World: How
     to Cross Boundaries, Build Bridges, and Lead Change*, Berrett-Koehler, Oakland,
     2015.

20   See Australian Civil-Military Centre and Australian Council for International
     Development, *Same Space—Different Mandates: A Civil-Military-Police Guide
     to Stakeholders in International Disaster and Conflict Response*, Commonwealth
     of Australia, 2015.; ACMC, Australian Government Guiding Principles for Civil-
     Military-Police Interaction in International Disaster and Conflict Management,
     2015, << https://www.acmc.gov.au/resources/publications/australian-government-
     guiding-principles-civil-military-police-interaction>> accessed 12 November
     2018.

21   Senate Standing Committee on Foreign Affairs, Defence and Trade, *Report of an
     Inquiry into Australia's Involvement in Peacekeeping Pperations*, 26 August 2008,
     Commonwealth of Australia 2008, p. 179.

CHAPTER 11

The enduring impact

Craig Stockings

In pondering the nation's response to the 1999 crisis in East Timor, it is well to cast our minds back some 20 years and remember the critical political and strategic circumstances of the crisis and the Australian Defence Force's contribution to it in the form of the International Force East Timor, or INTERFET. At its peak the INTERFET coalition deployed to East Timor was made up of contributions from 23 countries and numbered close to 11,000 military personnel. The force was led by an Australian, the then Major General Peter Cosgrove, and what equated, more or less, to an Australian headquarters. The ADF provided more than 9300 personnel to this coalition. It was the single biggest deployment of ADF personnel since the Second World War, larger than the commitment to the Vietnam War at its peak in 1967–68. Critically, it was a contribution not nestled within a lead nation's logistics or administrative infrastructure. Australia was not part of an American-led organisation which would be largely self-sustaining. It was also the first time Australia had led such a large multi-national force and all from a standing start.

In short, INTERFET was perhaps the most complex strategic challenge Australia had faced at least since the 1940s. Moreover, the operation proved to be one of the most successful United Nations (UN)-sanctioned peacemaking operations ever seen. Such a triumph had repercussions, both in East Timor and in Canberra. The INTERFET deployment was an activity that defined the career of its commander, Peter Cosgrove, and helped to shape the profile of John Howard's prime ministership. Many of the things that followed in the new millennium were essentially little more than aftershocks compared with how the Prime Minister emerged as a national security leader in 1999.

It is to some of these and other issues that I will focus upon in this chapter as the Official Historian of a multi-volume history series dealing with Australian involvement in Iraq (2003–11), Afghanistan (2001–14), and East Timor (1999–2012). The importance of this project speaks for itself. Australia's involvement in the Middle East has been complex and long-running. Well over 40,000 Australian Defence Force (ADF) and public service personnel served or supported these deployments over 13 years of operations. Sadly, 44 Australians died on active service in these theatres. Many hundreds more were wounded. The social, political and military effect of these conflicts globally, and within Australia, has been profound.

The official history series I am leading is the sixth produced by Australia. It continues a long and distinguished tradition begun by Charles Bean's work as general editor and principal author of the 15-volume *Official History of Australia in the War of 1914–18*. There is no question that each of the subsequent five official history series has faced their own specific challenges and enjoyed their own individual advantages. The effort to chronicle a wide range of ADF operations both near and far from Australian shores from 1999–2014 marks, however, an entirely new paradigm. This series is not, and could never be, a repeat of past experience that was merely updated for a new era. This is especially so given the sensitivities and security considerations associated with the unprecedented impact of intelligence and intelligence agencies on tactical military operations. It is also true of the mechanics of conducting research, noting the broader environment under which my team has laboured. It is less so in terms of the tradition and philosophy underlying past Australian official histories, which we are seeking to enhance.

A key difference between this series and those that have gone before is the type and level of governance imposed upon, and within, the project. I have been well-funded for this task and the team has enjoyed a level of resourcing not available to our predecessors. The obverse of deep government investment in the project is, however, an extremely tight timeline and reasonably rigid governance frameworks. My author teams were originally given five years to complete their volumes. This period was extended to six-and-a-half years early in 2018. This is a great deal less than has been available to any official history project to date. The Vietnam series, for instance, was completed over more than two decades.

My commission provides for controlled access to relevant government files and records, subject only to national security considerations. Though these volumes will be themselves unclassified, and written with this outcome in mind, they are based upon thorough study of the classified documentary record made available by the Government for the operations covered. Material excluded from the official history team and from publication, in whole or in part, is that judged by relevant government departments and agencies as potentially damaging to Australian continuing national security or national interests. Those agencies which have chosen to restrict their cooperation and access have done so on these grounds. I do not expect such omissions will alter the conclusions reached in the volume covering the INTERFET period in any discernable manner.

No series, official history or otherwise, can hope to capture all aspects and angles associated with the conflicts covered by these volumes. Thus, in all the volumes we have decided to focus our attention at the operational level. This is the space between tactical, individual and small-group activities on the ground and national strategic and political objectives being pursued by government and their departments. No volume in this series has attempted to detail the experiences or perspectives of Australian servicemen and servicewomen in the tradition of Charles Bean. Certainly, where context and opportunity allow, we will present the individual experiences of those deployed, but this is not our emphasis. While a noble and valuable endeavour, it is the subject of other works. These volumes aim to provide a comprehensive account of what Australian military units did and how they did it; and to explain and analyse the seminal choices made together with the implications for the operations under consideration. Further, these volumes concentrate on Australian activities. That is, while accepting the vital international setting of the conflicts covered in this series, the commentary is limited to providing sufficient context for Australian operations. How much is sufficient? There is no single measure and the amount will differ with each volume. I am expecting the volume authors to make a judgement in accordance with the requirement for careful and measured analysis. These volumes are scaffolded by as much material from 'above' and 'below' as the authors feel is needed to provide necessary context, dipping into the strategic and tactical as necessary.

The era when official military histories could be written almost exclusively from official Defence records has long passed. Like the operations they describe and analyse, such volumes as these have required input from whole-of-government sources. To this end, this series study is based not only on official Defence records but on documents sourced from a range of departments and agencies. In some instances, this record is not as complete as might be hoped given the speed of events, and the challenges posed for archiving by the growth of electronic media. Nor was the available body of records for the early volumes of this series helped by the fact that the period from 1999 to 2005 was in the middle of a transition from paper to electronic files in much Commonwealth government activity. In any case, such a record has been supplemented by extensive interviewing programs vital for getting behind what sometimes appears to be an artificial consensus of paperwork. Despite the whole-of-government reality of the operations covered in East Timor, Iraq and Afghanistan, and with due recognition of the many government and non-government agencies who were active in these theatres, these volumes must nonetheless—by necessity and mandate—centre on ADF operations. These volumes are therefore neither social histories, political histories, nor the record of Australians who voluntarily or at government behest deployed to these regions.

At their heart, the volumes of the official history are being written for those tens of thousands of Australians who deployed to these theatres from 1999–2014, and for the tens of thousands more that supported them on a professional level back home or who supported them personally with love and best wishes for a safe return. The series is also written to shed light on what happened, and why, for the wider Australian community who perhaps had only a brief or passing connection to the events at hand. It is further written, one hopes, for the interest and education of future generations who will benefit from knowing about East Timor's quest for independence, the long war against terrorism that began in Afghanistan, and the reasons for Iraqi society being upended. This series is, then, merely a start. It is an important foundation from which scholarship will grow, particularly as the documents upon which this study is based begin to be released for public consideration.

In terms of the volume concerned specifically with the East Timor crisis of 1999, and the enduring impact of these events, politicians, policy-makers and military officers at the very highest levels worried more about what might unfold as INTERFET deployed to Dili than about any other issue, at any other time in their careers beforehand or afterwards. East Timor was our backyard and the crisis into which it descended involved our most important northern neighbour. East Timor was also 'our' show. If it all went badly, and this was perceived at the time to constitute a real risk, the consequences were potentially disastrous for the nation in the medium and longer terms as well.

There is no question that as September 1999 approached, the high-level machinery of Australian national security was feeling the strain of a crisis it could not contain and into which Australia was being drawn. Faced with the looming reality of a direct military intervention in East Timor which was the antithesis of the long-standing political and diplomatic objectives of successive Australian governments, the atmosphere within the National Security Committee of Cabinet, for example, moved from tension to outright stress.

Relationships between key departments in Canberra were also unsettled. The relationship between the Minister for Foreign Affairs, Alexander Downer, and the Minister for Defence, John Moore, was less than cordial and, accordingly, less than effective. As the likelihood of military options took centre stage, the Department of Defence moved into the spotlight. The transition to Defence-led policy-making was not without its frictions with those more accustomed to setting the agenda at the departments of Foreign Affairs and Trade (Dfat) and of the Prime Minister and Cabinet (PM&C).

In short order, the NSC laid down four conditions that needed to be met before INTERFET might be executed. They were: Indonesian consent; United Nations (UN) authorisation; a clear endorsement of a significant proportion of Asean members; active American support and, more importantly, a guarantee for real military assistance should the deployment face serious challenge. Liaison with the Americans, however, got off to an unexpectedly shaky start. John Howard rang President Clinton on 6 September to discuss what specific assistance the United States might provide for any Australian-led intervention and to emphasise his personal preference for American boots on the ground. The Prime Minister was surprised at Clinton's reply. The President emphasised that the United States military was stretched beyond its limits and there was hostility within Congress to yet another overseas intervention. Alexander Downer was similarly stunned and allowed his disappointment to show in an interview screened on CNN. This disappointment led to a frank exchange of views with the United States Secretary of State, Madeleine Albright, with Downer again emphasising his dismay at the negative sounds emanating from Washington over American involvement and reiterating the material and symbolic value of United States' support. Policy-makers at the Pentagon took the point: Australia had been there for the United States in the past and was expected to be there in the future. It was time for some *quid pro quo.*

Soon afterwards, Washington did indeed confirm that all Australian requests were to be met. These requests included a commitment to 'backstop' the ADF if things got out of hand on the ground in East Timor but with the continuing caveat that American combat solders would not deploy. The NSC was briefed accordingly. It confirmed, once again, that it wanted a watertight guarantee that any resistance from Indonesia's armed forces would result in direct American intervention and it insisted on this message being relayed to Jakarta. The green light was given. Independently, and with no reference to the Pentagon, the United States Pacific Command devised plans to cover the withdrawal of a United Nations force from East Timor should a fight erupt with significant elements of the Indonesian military.

On 8 September, only 12 days from the force deploying, public statements made by government officials in Indonesia seemed to indicate that Jakarta would not accept a UN-sponsored intervention, thus removing one of the NSC's four conditions. Repeating a warning first given to international diplomats at the UN on 4 September, the Indonesian Foreign Minister, Ali Alatas, warned: 'Any nations willing to send peacekeepers to the province would have to shoot their way in'. This was followed by reports of Indonesia's Air Force chief warning that his forces were 'ready to face any intruders from Australia'. Planners and policy-makers within the Australian government correctly assumed that such sabre-rattling could not hold back the rising tide of international pressure. And, yet, serious conflict remained a terrifying possibility, especially if rogue elements of the Indonesian military defied political direction from Jakarta.

Nor were fears solely based on possible reactions from the Indonesian military. The self-styled militias in the province, with covert uniformed backing, were a threat in their own right. A draft press statement prepared for the Chief of the Defence Force, Admiral Chris Barrie, on 10 September, was clear in this regard. 'My information, based on eye-witness accounts from my own people, and other information sources', it read, 'is that militias armed with modern small arms have been conducting an orchestrated campaign of terror' with TNI support and cooperation in a monumental and 'blatant act of duplicity'. Meanwhile, militia leaders and anti-independence figures in the troubled province made predictions of their own. The Indonesian provincial governor, Jose Soares, for example, warned: 'If Australia sends a peacekeeping force we will be ready for them. There are thousands of us still—we will face them ... we will fight you when you arrive'. In Jakarta, one key adviser to President Habibie was reported in the Indonesian press as stating that Australian servicemen and servicewomen might be singled out for attack. She repeated the warning on the Australian SBS *Dateline* program on the evening of 15 September. Meanwhile, militia leaders like Eurico Guterres, later sentenced to ten years imprisonment for crimes against humanity, expressed their desire to exact a toll in blood on any foreign troops who entered the province.

Thus, for all the assumptions regarding outward Indonesian cooperation (or, at least, toleration) of the INTERFET landings, Australian planners could not discount the 'doomsday' scenario of a significant conflagration with the Indonesian military. Given the 'considerable evidence of cooperation' between the TNI and the militias, noted Minister for Defence, John Moore, 'one has to be prepared for any eventuality'. In an appreciation submitted to the NSC only 72 hours before the launch of INTERFET, the CDF assessed that while conventional Indonesian forces would likely cooperate to a degree and then be withdrawn, the militia groups, possibly backed by Special Forces, would likely try to test INTERFET's resolve. He also emphasised that the Government could not discount the possibility of a spiraling set of circumstances that might lead to armed conflict. Even though the Indonesians had agreed to an intervention, one argument ran, there was no guarantee that its own political leadership could fully control the instruments at the military's disposal. There was also little doubt that, in what would invariably be a charged environment in Dili upon landing, it might only take a small spark to ignite a serious incident 'accidentally'.

Meanwhile, Indonesian maritime and air force elements had begun to concentrate in West Timor and the surrounding area, ostensibly to facilitate a withdrawal of Indonesian forces from East Timor. Such movements included the placement on stand-by of F-16 (Fighting Falcon) and F-5 (Tiger) fighters, and the continuing deployment of a flight of BAE Hawk 100 and a pair of A-4 (Skyhawk) attack aircraft to Kupang. The Australian plan thus included an emergency exit criterion for an in-extremis evacuation of INTERFET. Such a scenario necessitated the landings be mounted with sufficient 'force protection', particularly in the air and at sea, to leave in as good an order as the force landed. Triggers for such a catastrophic event included the failure of the coalition, the failure of the mission, or the military defeat of INTERFET. The maintenance of air superiority and sea control, under such circumstances, was a daunting proposition and one assessed as requiring the maximum surge capacity of the ADF, along with multinational (United States) supplementation.

On the eve of INTERFET's arrival in Dili (19 September), the Prime Minister, John Howard, the Leader of the Opposition, Kim Beazley, the Leader of Australian Democrats, Meg Lees, the Minister for Defence, John Moore, and the CDF, Admiral Chris Barrie, gathered in Townsville to farewell the deploying personnel. The Prime Minister was emotional, well-aware of the uncertainty of what lay ahead. While the deployment of Special Air Service Regiment troops to Kuwait in 1998 had likely shaped Howard's thinking about the use of military force, and probably increased his confidence in doing so during his second term in office, INTERFET was an order of magnitude well beyond that decision. Howard himself later described the choice to deploy the ADF, on a scale of his toughest decisions, a nine-and-a-half out of ten: far and away the most significant decision his government had yet taken. He felt a great personal responsibility for the troops, a sense of anxiety for them, and for their families. After the formalities, politicians and senior ADF officers dined in the soldiers' mess, once more bringing home the personal aspects of the force about to be deployed. In a private moment the Prime Minister asked the Chief of Army, Lieutenant General Frank Hickling, if the task could be accomplished. 'I remember that very vividly', reflected Howard:

> I remember walking out with Jeannette and we saw the NCOs with groups of soldiers and we were talking to them and I remember thinking to myself: 'Gosh, some of them could be killed tomorrow'. That's how I felt ... it's the biggest thing you ever do ... You just think things can go wrong, and people can get killed, and you've sent them there.

For his part, Kim Beazley, himself a former long-serving Minister for Defence (1984–1990), noticed the quiet, sombre and reflective mood of troops who believed they were going into harm's way.

At the time, the fear of what might have gone wrong was profound for this nation's leaders, and for good reason. Even beyond the serious loss of life that would have accompanied even a short-term conflagration with the Indonesian military, the effect of such an event in the region would have been disastrous on multiple levels, most obviously on the diplomatic and economic fronts. Despite all the worry and all the sleepless night, INTERFET went well. Much was achieved at very little cost in human life or injury. As the deployment unfolded, broad smiles began to replace worried scowls. Much political capital was garnered after the fact. Decision-makers at a political level certainly emerged from the East Timor crisis of 1999–2000 with greater knowledge of, and perhaps confidence in, the application of military force than had previously been the case. To what degree such factors subsequently shaped decisions to employ the ADF at different times and in different theatres is, perhaps, impossible to measure. It is equally hard not to speculate. Just as it was for so many within the ADF, East Timor was the start rather than end of experiences with deployment for many senior decision-makers, right up to the prime minister. Had operations in East Timor not concluded successfully, it is not too much to wonder how much different more recent Australian military history might have been.

Political elites aside, I would argue that the East Timor crisis left an indelible mark on the wider Australian community. Remarkably, as events in the troubled province came to a climax in September 1999 with violent and destructive militia rampages, the Australian public demanded a military intervention to end the killing and the devastation of property. In an age of instant communications and the saturation of both traditional and internet reporting with images of the atrocities being perpetrated in Timor, the people, while mindful of the dangers, wanted action. This was a remarkable turnaround in public acceptance of the use of force and the deployment of Australian troops abroad. It was, perhaps, a signal of shifting attitudes among the post-Vietnam population or perhaps the nature of the event itself caused this change. Either way, the public clamour for something decisive to happen could not have been lost on politicians and policy-makers.

Domestic pressure associated with how and when the Government should react to the situation in East Timor beyond the relatively simple issue of evacuations ramped up exponentially and in direct proportion to the dramatic upturn in violence during the first week of September. The terrible crimes in the province were comprehensively reported by the Australian media and such images created public outrage throughout the nation. Most often this outrage took the form of calls to deploy the ADF immediately, from talk-back radio to Opposition taunting. All major newspapers argued for immediate Australian involvement. The Prime Minister's staff were flooded by letters from state politicians, religious leaders, interest groups, union organisations and private citizens. The situation was the same in John Moore's office. It was inundated with public calls for action across the full spectrum of the community, from school children to retirees. In response to a deluge of parliamentary questions, the Minister for Foreign Affairs, Alexander Downer, could only exasperatedly repeat that the Australian Government was making strong representations to Jakarta about the continuing violence, and that any deployment of peacekeepers was dependent on Indonesian agreement. A deployment in advance of formal agreements would have been, in Howard's words, 'tantamount to declaring war'. Although entirely true, these were increasingly unsatisfactory answers for an Australian people and press shocked by what they were witnessing.

As each day ticked by, images of the razing of Dili and the suffering of the East Timorese assailed Australians on nightly news programs. The crisis became the subject of heated conversations in cafes and over dinner tables. A *Sydney Morning Herald* editorial of 8 September represented what was rapidly becoming a public consensus: 'the immediate and urgent question is what must be done to stop further crimes'. The editorial ventured: 'the short answer is whatever it takes'. The previous day demonstrators outside DFAT's Northern Territory office called for an immediate dispatch of peacekeepers. Around 1000 more repeated the performance outside DFAT's office in

Melbourne. Public rallies had begun in Sydney as early as 6 September when East Timorese activists and several hundred trade unionists protested outside the Sydney office of Garuda Airlines (Indonesia's national airline), calling for the deployment of a multi-national force. Two days later a much larger rally was held in the city with around 4000 city workers walking off their job sites to join it. The union movement was prominent in these actions. Garbage workers in Sydney, for example, with the support of Randwick Council, refused to collect rubbish from the Indonesian Consulate. Similarly, printing workers refused to print Indonesian products while the Maritime Union of Australia prevented the loading of cargo on all Indonesia-bound ships.

The union movement was by no means the only point of pressure. Another vocal source of public advocacy for intervention was the Roman Catholic Church. During one particular meeting with a group of influential religious figures, Howard was again forced to point out that while he appreciated their position and shared their outrage, an Australian military intervention in East Timor without UN sanction and Indonesian approval was an act of war. Public agitation, however, continued to escalate. A rally on Saturday 11 September which began in Hyde Park with about 15,000 attendees eventually ended with around double that number. It was a similar situation in Melbourne where approximately 30,000 people rallied in the city on short notice on 10 September and a further 40,000 gathered in a march on Sunday 19 September. The Australian public grew ever more strident in its demands for action, including use of the ADF.

Civic activism did not force the Government's hands on the issue. The movement towards a deployment was well advanced before the rallies gained momentum. But they were crucial background music for Australian politicians who did not have to look hard or very far to predict the political consequences of not taking decisive action. Moreover, it was the breadth of public pressure, coming from such a wide spectrum of the community, that drew and held political attention.

Conversely, after INTERFET arrived on 20 September and brought an end to the rampages, the enduring public images and the essence of the public memory was not of strategic judgements and political calculations, policy enigmas, operational missteps or even the horrific results of what I would call the 'militia strategy'. Rather, the images and memories that lingered were of the locals—families rebuilding their lives amidst the rubble that had been bequeathed to them and smiling children. The feeling of helping a desperate and grateful people was what INTERFET veterans brought home with them. This was the principal achievement. Beyond all else said or written about Australian operations in East Timor in this period, this is the legacy that will endure.

The Chief of Army, Lieutenant General Frank Hickling, told a parliamentary committee in June 2000 that 'the final lesson we do need to absorb, not only as an army but as a society, is that the INTERFET operation was not war'. But East Timor felt like victory from initial deployment to welcome home parade. To what extent, then, did this experience shape the Australian community's attitude to, and acceptance of, the use of Australian military power abroad in the early years of the new millennium? To what degree were lingering fears and protracted suspicions of deploying Australian troops overseas—fears older than Federation—allayed by INTERFET's accomplishments? To follow this line of thinking: how much did such feelings feed into subsequent politico-diplomatic-military calculations? East Timor was only the start of a hectic operational period for the ADF but it was an important start. If the ADF had received a bloody nose in 1999, would subsequent deployments still have happened? This question remains.

Another important aspect of the East Timor crisis needs to be borne in mind. The ADF operation in East Timor was not the product of a considered and long-term strategic planning and policy process. It was actually a failure of that process. To be blunt, there was a chasm between what the Coalition Government wanted to achieve in East Timor in late 1998 and what was actually achieved by February 2000. Australian policy-makers never wanted nor sought East Timorese independence in 1999. The choice was made for them. Events set in motion during the final months of 1998 were not at all what Canberra had hoped for. On the contrary, the chain of events leading to East Timorese independence was born out of what Australian policy-makers perceived as a moment or window of opportunity, created by the fall of President Suharto, to legitimise the continuing incorporation of East Timor into Indonesia. Doing so would remove the 'burr under the saddle' in the bi-lateral relationship, and diminish the international stigma generated by Indonesia's occupation of the territory. This stigma was carefully, stubbornly and successfully husbanded by East Timorese lobby groups around the globe for 25 years. The tears of joy shed by locals in Dili as INTERFET was deployed represented, on one level, a significant Australian policy reversal. There has been, noted one former and very senior official from DFAT, 'a lot of sort of post-event re-writing of history ... about Australia being the "liberator" of East Timor'. In 1998, he continued, 'being the "liberator" of East Timor was the last thing on our minds'.

Indeed, from an Australian perspective, a diplomatic initiative designed to improve the bilateral relationship with Indonesia did precisely the opposite. A series of events was triggered that reduced relations between the two nations to their lowest point since the Indonesia-Malaysia Confrontation of the mid-1960s. The Indonesian military was subjected to international ignominy as a new but poor nation came into existence that threated the all-important strategic 'arc of stability' to the north of the Australian continent. If DFAT had written a script late in 1998 as to what a disaster scenario might look like regarding East Timor in a post-Suharto era, perhaps only an outright war over the territory between Australia and Indonesia would have been worse than what transpired in the second half of 1999.

It was worse in many ways because Australian diplomats and policy-makers had brought this on themselves. Only a week into the INTERFET deployment, Prime Minister Howard told the House of Representatives that 13 years of predominantly Labor Party foreign policy failure and neglect had, more than anything else, created the crisis in East Timor. Furthermore, over the previous 25 years, he believed governments of both political persuasions had got it wrong in relation to Australia's policy on East Timor. He included himself in this criticism with the inference that things were now being put to right. While no doubt such sentiments were sincere, they did not match the policy position or practical actions taken in Canberra in the tumultuous lead-up to the INTERFET deployment. Indeed, a very senior Defence official conceded, 'the government-endorsed public narrative was not the real historical narrative.'

None of this commentary is intended to cast moral or ethical judgement on government policy or official actions. All participants, as far as might be judged, operated in good faith but that faithfulness ought to be understood in terms of what was perceived as very much a realist interpretation of

Australia's national interests. There was no conspiracy in Canberra, no cabal of faceless bureaucrats twisting policy to their own ends. Instead, there was a powerful consensus that Australia's interests were best served by the stability and security provided by a strong Indonesia which incorporated East Timor. Australia would benefit most from a strong bi-lateral relationship between Canberra and Jakarta. East Timor was either a distraction or an obstruction to pursuing that diplomatic end. Most senior diplomats were adamant on this point. This was not a novel view. It reflected powerful generational outlooks and a dominant orthodoxy. Whether or not you agree with that consensus, its logic stands.

Importantly, after INTERFET had run its course, the politics of what led to its creation continued to rankle many veterans. At one level, most understood the practical need to reestablish as close and cooperative a relationship with Jakarta as soon as possible. For many, an unsettled feeling remained nonetheless. Thousands of Australian servicemen and servicewomen saw with their own eyes what had unfolded in East Timor and who had been responsible. Hundreds of their more senior officers and non-commissioned officers with access to intelligence summaries and collected observations knew this in some depth. Dozens of high-ranking officers in East Timor and back in Australia, along with their civilian counterparts across multiple agencies, knew that the post-referendum rampage was likely if not inevitable. Nearly 20 years later, those involved are almost unanimous in their assessments of how the violence in East Timor was perpetrated and who was responsible. They can even name those who deserved to be indicted. At the time, ADF members did not need to reconcile any of the philosophical or political issues; they just needed to get on with the job. With the passage of time and on deeper reflection, however, many veterans have felt discomfort about the questions that no-one in 1999 wanted to ask let alone answer.

For his part, Prime Minister Howard personally drew very important lessons from the East Timor crisis. These lessons spoke to the heart of previous policy consistencies. He asserted: 'this country over the last 20 years—that's Australia—has had far too many special relationships and it's a phrase that's dropped all too readily from the lips of too many prime ministers.' East Timor had 'driven home to us the foolishness of building a foreign policy on the notion of special relationships, and the compatibility of temperaments and personalities of the leaders of nation at any given period.'

How this newfound attitude meshed with personal and policy conviction in the wake of the September 11 attacks upon the US is an interesting question and one left to another time.

Finally, what of East Timor's enduring influence upon the ADF as an organisation and the wider national security apparatus? The crisis was without question a crucible that both tested and reshaped the way Australia dealt with its national security concerns. The NSC, ministers, various intelligence agencies and a range of government departments, not just Defence, gained much valuable experience as a result of the intervention. New systems and structures were put in place and new pecking orders emerged. The relationship between Defence and DFAT, for example, embraced a fresh equilibrium. Critics called it a 'militarisation' of foreign policy; advocates thought it was merely confirmation that the military could be used as an instrument of strategic policy rather than being something separate from it, or entirely subordinate to it. So, too, the agencies of the Australian intelligence community found the distinctions between operational and strategic intelligence were fast disappearing. Intelligence capabilities previously regarded as strategic and largely managed by civilians were used to provide direct operational support to the ADF, which required operational adjustments and a redefinition of roles and functions. This 'operationalisation' of traditionally strategic agencies began during the East Timor operation and continued well into the future.

From an ADF-specific viewpoint, even beyond the overall success of operations in East Timor, there was much about which to be satisfied. The true measure of military effectiveness is, of course, the outcome. The Defence establishment gave the Government what it wanted. The sense of quiet determination at all levels from an organisation with so little operational experience was impressive. The plaudits were well-deserved. Behind the scenes, the events of 1999 rocked the Department of Defence and the ADF to their core. As a consequence of the international context of this deployment, overt American posturing, and decisions made by the Indonesian Government and the Indonesian military prior to 20 September, operations culminating in the INTERFET deployment never came close to failure, largely because they were not challenged. The ADF did not stumble in East Timor because it was never seriously pushed. The process of mounting these operations, however, even in a largely uncontested environment, exposed the organisation to scrutiny and tested it like no peacetime exercise possibly could. In the process, the costs of the long post-Vietnam peace were exposed. ADF resources were severely stretched and a yawning gap between advertised and actual capability was revealed. The deployment to East Timor imposed critical limitations on the size, scale and scope of other contingency responses that could be mounted by the ADF. It took until July 2000 for INTERFET units to be considered reconstituted and re-deployable. This was a significant constraint upon the ADF's flexibility and its capacity to meet any other short-notice, offshore contingency.

The biggest obstacle the ADF faced in planning and executing INTERFET was itself. The organisation had become hollow since the 1970s and found that it was profoundly unsuited to a large-scale operation overseas of the magnitude demanded by the East Timor crisis. This was especially true of the Australian Army and deployable ground elements of the Air Force (less so the flying squadrons or the Navy). It was much more than the mere fact the ADF had not dispatched a military force of this size since the 1960s. The ADF had, according to the 1987 'Defence of Australia' doctrine, been actively structuring itself in a manner that would impede its ability to deploy for a Timor-style operation. In parallel, it sponsored a string of 'efficiency' initiatives designed to save money in the context of a Defence Force that was not seen to need a significant expeditionary capability. Defence had shaved its capabilities to match available funding. The Defence Efficiency Review alone reduced the RAAF from 16,500 personnel to 13,000 men and women with these reductions taking effect early in 1999.

A further issue, only partly explained by the funding environment of the late 1980s and 1990s, was the ADF's own culture and the habits it sustained. The organisation never practised mounting an operation overseas on such a scale; it only rehearsed what it would do once in-theatre. It had neither exercised nor evaluated connectivity or interoperability between the strategic, the operational and the tactical levels of command. It therefore failed to develop or test enabling functions, particularly of the newer 'joint' ADF organisations and capabilities.

Many of the ADF's INTERFET planning problems from late August 1999 were simply a consequence of its lack of practice. Confused command and control lines meant sluggish response times down the chain of command. Orders and instructions arrived too late to influence tactical-level preparations. Critically, until 1999 only lip service had been paid to the importance of logistics planning and materiel support in any of the large ADF exercises. Deficiencies therefore remained hidden and capability gaps were glossed over. In the words of one senior officer: 'We were not prepared for it', he conceded, 'we were not exercised for it, we were not trained for it.'

The bottom line was that the outcome for the ADF in East Timor was a success in spite of some potentially serious impediments. It succeeded due to the quality and determination of its people who endured failures of process and systems. A combination of the outstanding successes of ADF operations in East Timor in 1999, and the simultaneous exposure of some critical problems and weaknesses, revealed a very important set of lessons and legacies. As a result of corporate soul-searching, many of the issues and shortfalls identified were addressed in the following years. Even before INTERFET had concluded, the Minister for Defence, John Moore, announced increasing numbers of uniformed specialists in construction, intelligence, and logistics, and plans to expand ADF capabilities to match the demonstrable shortfalls.

Perhaps most importantly in this regard was the release of the 2000 Defence White Paper. It was a watershed document that acknowledged an expeditionary role for the ADF and foreshadowed the work that was needed to ensure there would be no repeat of the problems in 1999. It marked a shift away from 'Defence of Australia' concepts that focused attention on the air-sea gap to the north of the Australian continent to a strategic model that focused on increasing stability in the 'inner arc' of nations that bordered Australia in the Indo-Pacific.

Specifically, the ADF was to contribute effectively to international coalitions of forces to meet crises beyond Australia's immediate neighbourhood. To achieve this capacity, ADF numbers were to be increased from its current strength of 51,500 to around 54,000 full-time members by 2010. Funding for 2001–02 and 2002–03 was commensurately programmed to increase by AUD$500 million and AUD$1000 million respectively. Unsurprisingly, emphasis was on training, equipping and sustaining a brigade group offshore for an extended period. At the same time, the ADF would make at least a battalion group available for deployment elsewhere. This was the challenge that had been so difficult during the INTERFET period.

The cultural impact of INTERFET and other ADF operations in East Timor was similarly profound. With the exception of a small number of high-readiness units, an essentially peacetime or peace-oriented ADF was shaken suddenly from slumber. Old assumptions were contested and emerging philosophies explored. The INTERFET mission was, for instance, the first time Australian women were operationally deployed in large numbers on active service. At its height, this number approached around 420 of 5500, a high percentage, although one still lower than the overall proportion of women within the ADF at that time. So, too, the Australian Special Forces component during INTERFET emerged with a greatly enhanced reputation among the upper echelons of ADF command. As the Chief of Army and then as the Chief of the Defence Force, General Peter Cosgrove oversaw a significant expansion and enhancement of the Special Forces community, culminating in the raising of Special Operations Command in May 2003. In itself, this process changed the nature, structure and culture of both the Army and the ADF. Again, however, the process must be understood within the context of continuing operations in the Middle East and Afghanistan. The crisis in East Timor ought to be seen as the starting point for the complex processes and complicated operations that unfolded for the ADF in the years that followed.

How do these observations shape the current official history series? In terms of an organising philosophy, my approach differs very little from my predecessors. Official histories are, in many ways, a record of government actions and decisions based on government sources. They are not government stories, however, or means by which certain narratives might be perpetuated at the expense of others. They are the product of historical investigations by independent researchers. The government pays the bill but it does not determine what is written.

Official histories provide a foundation and offer a framework for future historians, and an accessible way for the public and the veteran community to gain insight into the operations and theatres under examination. This is particularly important given prevailing perceptions of a severe disconnect between the conduct of these 'wars' and the Australian people. My colleagues and I need to address what might be described as mismatches between the public narrative of events in East Timor, Iraq and Afghanistan, and the historical evidence at hand. Our outlook has been straightforward. We have not self-censored. We have included the good with the bad. Frictions and mistakes are as valid a part of the historical record as tactical victories and operational successes. Achievements in spite of institutional shortcomings tend to enhance the legacy of those involved, not the reverse. We have written the history as we have seen it and as the evidence trail has led us. These volumes aim, therefore, to be truthful and not triumphal. The enduring impact of these works, beginning with the first East Timor volume, will be a matter for future historians to judge.

POSTSCRIPT

Lessons learned and insights acquired

Tom Frame

There is much to be gained by institutions and individuals marking the passage of time. It is a means of charting progress and regress in human affairs, comparing one period to another and then contrasting rates of change, or assessing individual advancement towards a desired goal. Significant anniversaries—often featuring years ending in zero, such as tenth, fiftieth and hundredth anniversaries— are moments to reflect on events and experiences and to extract whatever wisdom hindsight might offer. Lessons from the past may not have been fully understood or applied correctly. Alternatively, there may be insights that have eluded the gaze of those who might learn from them. Some things happen so quickly or with such profound effect that their importance is neither perceived nor felt for decades.

The twentieth anniversary of the INTERFET deployment in September 2019 prompted timely reflection on the end of Indonesia's annexation of East Timor and the start of Timor-Leste's life as an independent nation. It was also a critical moment in history for the Australian Defence Force (ADF), the Australian Federal Police (AFP) and the Australian Public Service (APS). The East Timor crisis showed each organisation how rapidly their operational environments were evolving and the extent of the change that was required in meeting present needs and emerging demands. The contributors to this collection reveal that the crisis challenged the experience and expertise of even the most accomplished leaders. The twists and turns that accompanied the implosion of civil society in East Timor required an intervention for which very few people were prepared or were prepared adequately.

It is always difficult to be ready for situations involving volatile human nature. People behave in unpredictable ways when under stress, whether prompted by anger or fear. The pro-Indonesian political factions and their locally armed militias knew ahead of the formal ballot that the independence vote would probably prevail. Destroying Jakarta's infrastructure investments and damaging the institutions that sustained community life made absolutely no sense. East Timor was their home. Most did not want to live elsewhere. And yet they laid waste to everything that would make a better life possible for themselves once the Indonesians left. The destruction was mindless and the killing was pointless. It exceeded the sanguine expectations of commentators and the careful predictions of analysts who thought reprisals were likely. The vengeful rage that demonstrated complete indifference to the sanctity of human life and respect for private property exceeded the worst fears of what might happen among the best informed observers. That so much of the violence seemed ordered and targeted suggested much deeper complicity from the deeply resentful Indonesian military. This was a dark hour for them; their standing diminished and their reputation tarnished.

In contrast to the militia rampages late in August and early in September 1999, the intervention did not result in substantial loss of life for those who deployed nor among those who resented, and then resisted, their presence. But things could have been so much worse. From December 1998 when Prime Minister Howard wrote to President Habibie about the future of East Timor until May 2002 when Timor-Leste declared its independence, there was every possibility that the transfer of sovereignty from Jakarta to Dili could have produced enduring problems for Indonesia, Timor-Leste, Australia and the Asia-Pacific region.

Indonesia's government, and eventually its people, accepted the desire of the East Timorese to pursue a future that did not involve Jakarta's political oversight. The 'loss' of East Timor as its 27th province did not destabilise the Indonesian state nor did it cause any economic hardship to ordinary Indonesians. East Timor had detracted from Indonesia's standing as a nation on the world stage and it had been a drain on the republic's finances. Patriotic pride was certainly depleted because the need for foreign intervention could only be seen by the Indonesian people as public humiliation. Neither the Indonesian military nor its police were either willing or able to constrain the behaviour of unruly, anti-democratic thugs. That Indonesia could not deal with an internal law and order issue implied it was not yet an advanced nation-state that was capable of dealing competently with its own affairs. That it needed the 'assistance' of nations like Australia and Thailand was, to many of its people, an affront to their national dignity.

A handful of Indonesians imbued with anti-Western hatred responded with religiously-inspired violence. It was directed principally at Australia. In 2002, 88 Australians were among the 202 people killed by the terrorist bombing of two popular nightclubs at Kuta Beach in Bali. Australians were the main target in an attack purportedly committed as revenge for Canberra's interference in East Timor (and for participating in the 2001 invasion of Afghanistan). Relations between Indonesia and Australia were certainly strained for a number of years although there was nothing new in the existence of tension between the two nations. This particular rift was repaired with resumption of the Indonesia-Australia Ministerial Dialogue in March 2003 and the ADF's much appreciated involvement in disaster relief on Indonesian soil after the Boxing Day 2004 tsunami and the subsequent earthquake between the islands of Nias and Simeulue.

Timorese independence leaders, such as José Ramos-Horta, commented in the mid-1990s that East Timor needed a decade of assisted autonomy before being ready for full independence. When self-determination was offered to the East Timorese in August 1999, however, they collectively seized the opportunity to express themselves. Whatever the political or the practical benefits of longer preparation for independence, and these benefits should not be underestimated, the East Timorese plainly wanted to be free of Indonesian oppression without any further delay. Neither Ramos-Horta nor his close colleague, Xanana Gusmão, asked the Indonesians to delay the United Nations (UN) sponsored plebiscite held in August 1999. It might not have been an optimal arrangement but they accepted the opportunity for self-expression nonetheless. Although Timor-Leste was, and remains, an economically poor country, it is a nation that is free to determine its own affairs and to chart its own future. In 1999 the people preferred the offer of immediate political freedom to the appeal of eventual administrative efficiency.

Relations between Australia and Timor-Leste since it gained independence in May 2002 have been marked by close cooperation and bitter conflict, the latter arising from disagreements over joint exploration of oil and gas reserves in the Timor Sea. Australia has consistently been the largest bi-lateral aid donor (exceeding $1 billion) and has undergirded a number of emerging state institutions, including the Timor-Leste defence force. There have been high level ministerial talks and the establishment of a Timor-Leste Embassy in Canberra with consulates in all state capitals. For the foreseeable future, Timor-Leste remains dependent on foreign aid, mainly from Australia, to support infrastructure development and the protection of national assets. Indonesia has become Timor-Leste's principal trading partner and its foremost advocate for admission to the Association of South East Asian Nations (ASEAN). When viewed from 2019, much that is positive and productive has come from the events of 1999. Australia certainly became aware of its limitations as a nation.

The contributors to this volume have set out what they, and the organisations they led, learned from what happened twenty years ago. They have also explained why those who were involved in managing the crisis deserve credit for their enduring achievements. In the minds of most Australians, the intervention was a national triumph. INTERFET and East Timor overshadowed the effectiveness of contemporaneous missions in Bougainville (1998–2003) and the Solomon Islands (2003–17). INTERFET was also cited internationally as an example of an effective peacekeeping mission that was sanctioned by the United Nations but neither organised nor led by it. Australia has been praised for bringing together a coalition of like-minded nations that were quickly able to operate effectively to protect human rights and pursue regional stability. Australian uniformed and civilian personnel, together with diplomatic officers, were praised for their personal qualities and professional prowess. There was a widely-held view that Australia could be trusted to exercise diplomatic leadership in Asia-Pacific security affairs after its contribution to the Asian financial crisis in 1997 had revealed its capacity for economic leadership.

Other than inevitable, and perhaps unavoidable, difficulties with Indonesia over the end of its near universally contested annexation of the former Portuguese colony, the role played by Australia was a highly creditable one. Even so, a number of commentators have criticised John Howard's claim that the intervention was one of his government's foremost achievements, ranking in merit alongside the reform of Australia's gun laws following the 1996 Port Arthur massacre and the elimination of the country's very substantial accumulated public debt. These criticisms are not atypical of broader attempts to diminish the Howard Government's record during its time in office. But what of the specifics in this instance? An example of early criticism (2003) was an article by the former Australian Ambassador to Indonesia (at the time of the 1975 invasion), Richard Woolcott, who went much further than questioning the validity of Howard's claiming credit for East Timor's liberation. He referred to Howard's would-be 'noble' act as one of sheer folly.[1] Woolcott attributed to Howard the worst kind of motive in dealing with East Timor: the creation and then exploitation of a foreign policy crisis for domestic political gain.

According to Woolcott, Howard thought he could 'engineer a regional diplomatic success' by leveraging President BJ Habibie's volatile personality to his own advantage. After shadow foreign affairs spokesman, Laurie Brereton, was critical of previous Australian policy on East Timor in August 1998, Woolcott alleged that it suited Howard 'to promote the theory that the Whitlam, Hawke and Keating Governments had behaved immorally and improperly in the 1970s, 1980s and 1990s'. Howard himself did not make any such claim. He could hardly criticise previous governments when his own had embraced the Hawke-Keating line during its first two years in office. Howard also conceded his own support for the previous policy, including during the Fraser years when he was a Cabinet minister. (He was Treasurer from 1977 to 1983).

Howard was also largely indifferent to the partisan potential of Brereton's statement. In fact, Howard did not even need bi-partisan support to change his own party's policy given the prevailing mood of the Australian people which was firmly behind East Timorese independence. Howard was not, as Woolcott claims, 'a belated supporter of self-determination in East Timor and of what he is prone to call true Australian values'. He was actually a convert to the cause of independence and said so publicly. Howard went further: it was 'right' for Australia to change its policy after the East Timorese had endured more than two decades of oppression by Indonesia.

Pursuing the theme of 'folly', Woolcott thought it was 'unwise' for Howard to write to Habibie, 'given Habibie's temperament', because such a letter would likely be used to precipitate action that Woolcott believed was premature. Woolcott claimed that Habibie 'knew very little' about East Timor, was poorly advised and should have been dissuaded from offering the East Timorese independence before they were ready. Woolcott was personally critical of the Indonesian president and his ministers: 'that such a major decision could be taken without full consideration and with such limited discussion by an impatient, erratic interim president can only be regarded as irresponsible'. Woolcott thought a phased transition to independence would have been cheaper in the longer term than the cost of ending 'the spiteful devastation' that followed the independence ballot in 1999. He seemed to think violence would have been averted if the eventual end of Indonesian rule had been announced earlier, dismissing the possibility that the violence would have been more protracted if the pro-Indonesian factions had been allowed to organise themselves earlier.

Surprisingly, given his previous criticism, Woolcott could 'accept that Howard and Foreign Affairs Minister Alexander Downer believed that what they did was right in the circumstances as they interpreted them; but the road to hell is sometimes paved with good intentions'. This is a strange argument. Did Woolcott want Howard and Downer to ignore any sense of what was right and persist with a policy that they believed was wrong? Or should the consequences determine whether an action is deemed right or wrong? This suggests either political opportunism or moral cowardice. To chide the Howard Government for 'evangelical altruism' is unworthy of someone of Woolcott's standing in the diplomatic community.

Woolcott further claimed that a number of regional leaders were critical of Howard for precipitating a crisis in East Timor although each of these nations later contributed to the intervention. He alleged that Australia's approach to the ballot and the intervention was 'excessively assertive, jingoistic and triumphalist' whereas Australian diplomacy would have been 'more effective and would have generated less animosity in Indonesia and our neighbourhood if we had been less prominent, more persuasive, less insistent on taking the lead and less demanding in pursuing our objectives'. These criticisms are fanciful. They are based on dissent that Woolcott magnifies for the purpose of detracting from the Howard Government's achievements. He also gives Australia's neighbours more credit for a consistent and coherent policy on East Timor than actually existed among them at the time. Most of them had little interest in East Timor or its independence struggle. It was, to them, a matter of minor concern.

As Howard and Downer both noted in 1998, Woolcott was part of the dominant faction in the Australian diplomatic community that was preoccupied with maintaining Jakarta's goodwill at all costs. Woolcott, and his like-minded colleagues, wanted to avoid any disagreement with Indonesia over the mere 'side-show' that was East Timor. Woolcott claimed Australia's neighbours thought Canberra's focus on East Timor was 'excessive and unbalanced'. More important in a regional sense, he contended, was Indonesia's 'successful transition to a more stable, moderate, representative government, the recovery of the Indonesian economy, and a willingness to deal with extremist Islamist organisations'. The worst outcome was the uncertainty produced by the Howard Government's policy:

> At best we may see in the future an economically struggling, quasi-democratic state with a benign relationship with its larger neighbour, Indonesia. But there is a danger that we could find ourselves supporting indefinitely a factionalised, unstable mini-state characterised by chronic dependency and ongoing problems with Indonesia.

His foreboding was mistaken. Likewise, the quip made by an unnamed 'senior member of the present Bush Administration' who told Woolcott that 'East Timor will be your Haiti'. Woolcott ended flippantly: 'Australians can only hope he is wrong'.

Not only is Woolcott's assessment little more than a partisan lament lacking balance and fair-mindedness, time has revealed the inaccuracy of his assertions. Australia's relationship with Indonesia returned to its previous good health and Timor-Leste's achievements have surpassed the worst fears of doomsayers. Its democracy has faltered at times and its economy is weak but it has not been an intolerable burden to Australia nor become a distraction for Indonesia. The 1999 crisis produced many positive benefits and none of the diplomatic disasters that Woolcott predicted.

More recently (2019), detractors of the Howard Government's achievement in East Timor have drawn on declassified official records from 1998–99. The ABC's Indonesia correspondent, Anne Barker, claimed that

> newly published intelligence documents declassified by the United States … suggest Australia did not support or plan for a peacekeeping mission in Timor-Leste until the last minute … [and] that it was the United States—and not Australia—that ultimately forced Indonesia to accept peacekeepers into the country and uphold the referendum result … Nowhere in the documents is there any sign that Australia actively pressured the United States to take steps to protect the Timorese, despite the worsening violence.[2]

Barker claimed that these documents dispelled John Howard's narrative that the 'liberation' of Timor was among his proudest moments as prime minister. Not only, Barker claims, had he supported the continuation of Indonesia's occupation of East Timor, he had 'consistently lobbied against the deployment of peacekeepers'. This argument has been around since 2004 when my UNSW colleague, Clinton Fernandes, published *Reluctant Saviour: Australia, Indonesia and the Independence of East Timor*.[3]

John Howard did not reply to the assertions in Barker's story but his former Minister for Foreign Affairs, Alexander Downer, did. He stated bluntly, these 'assertions are totally wrong'. He told Barker:

> there is a long record of Australian commentary on these events. We never lobbied against a peacekeeping force and you seem totally unaware of the huge effort we made in 1999 to stem the violence in East Timor—including the Bali summit with President [BJ] Habibie … As for the Americans, perhaps you are unaware of the difficulty we had in getting [President Bill] Clinton and [National Security Advisor Samuel 'Sandy'] Berger engaged to help at any stage.

Barker did not explain to her readers that her story was based on American documents, that they did not provide either a comprehensive or consistent portrayal of the unfolding crisis. Also absent was any mention that the United States only agreed to play a part in the resolution of the crisis when John Howard personally and Alexander Downer publicly expressed the deep disappointment of the Australian Government that Washington had failed to fulfil an Australian request for assistance in a manner consistent with Canberra's response to American pleas for help over a number of decades. It was in this context that the Commander of United States Forces in the Pacific, Admiral Dennis Blair, conveyed to General Wiranto the clear message that the United States would not tolerate any interference with INTERFET's mission and that it would contribute ground forces were there any resistance. Blair conveyed a threat, nothing more. The mission was already underway. It was not initiated or made possible by the United States. Direct American involvement was a last resort and a reasonably remote one.

Further, both Howard and Downer were constrained at that time from commenting on the conduct of the TNI and the pro-Indonesian militias for two reasons. The first was the risk of revealing that Canberra was closely monitoring confidential communications between Dili and Jakarta. The extent of this knowledge will be revealed in the forthcoming official history. Second, they wanted to avoid alienating the leaders of Indonesia's military to whom they were appealing personally for action in restraining the violence. There were no grounds for any Australian political leader either to defend or to excuse the actions of Indonesian military personnel or their surrogates in East Timor. There were, however, solid grounds for pursuing constructive dialogue with President Habibie and Foreign Minister Ali Alatas in resolving the continuing difficulties that East Timor posed for Australian-Indonesian relations and managing the crisis that followed the independence ballot.

Speaking candidly about the intervention on the twentieth anniversary of the deployment, both Howard and Downer expressed surprise that in 1999 a range of otherwise informed commentators, some from the political left, urged the Australian Government to take direct action in East Timor and to ignore the reaction of the Indonesian Government. Such action would have precipitated a wider conflict with Indonesia. As Alatas remarked on 8 September 1999, any international peacekeeping force would have to 'shoot its way into East Timor'. He was adamant that Jakarta would not bow to ultimatums even as he tried to explain away the indefensible actions of his nation's military and the militias they were inciting to violence. Although the Howard Government was later accused of being too willing to use force in the invasions of Afghanistan in 2001 and Iraq in 2003, this was an instance when reticence was interpreted as weakness. It was much more a case of adopting cautious restraint as an organising principle while planning for an intervention, initially in the form of evacuating foreign nationals, and preparing for whatever contingencies followed the independence ballot.

Assessing whether John Howard and his government is entitled to claim credit for East Timor's liberation is a more complex activity than simply assembling a series of counterclaims and criticisms. His government initially maintained Labor's policy on the annexation and continued to negotiate with Indonesia on matters relating to its 27th province. The Coalition's policy was influenced by what the end of the Suharto regime meant for East Timor and, to a much lesser degree, the shift in Labor's view and Brereton's public denunciation of its previous position. Howard was aware that diplomatic and political circumstances had changed, that the East Timorese were facing intolerable oppression that needed to end, and that Australia ought to 'do what was right' in the face of enduring injustice.

The previous approach may have been morally egregious despite its diplomatic appeal and practical benefits but the decision was made in 1998 to support the promotion of East Timorese autonomy and eventually independence. This was not without risks to Australia economically and the Coalition politically. Within three years, the East Timorese achieved independence—something that was unthinkable throughout 1997 and for the first half of 1998. The transition from annexation to sovereignty was never going to happen without conflict as there was much at stake for the Indonesians and the East Timorese. Resolving the conflict could have been worse, much worse. It happened much more quickly that Howard and his ministers had imagined but this might have proved a better option in the longer term. We will never know. While critics might be reluctant to grant John Howard and his government credit for East Timor's liberation, he deserves to be recognised for assembling and deploying Australia's diverse national assets and its like-minded international partners under the banner of INTERFET to address a long-standing human tragedy. Future commentary on East Timor between 1998 and 2001 needs to transcend the partisan spirit that has led to unbalanced assessments of where criticism and congratulation ought to be directed.

As Australians debated the entitlement of the Howard Government to claim 'credit' for resolving the 1999 crisis, the people of Timor-Leste celebrated their liberation from Portuguese colonialism and Indonesian imperialism. A large twentieth anniversary party was at held at Tasi Tolu, the 'three lakes', on the edge of the capital Dili. Many of the youthful revelers had no personal experience of Indonesian rule. With more than half of its citizens aged under 20, Timor-Leste has one of the world's youngest populations. Nevertheless, stories from the 1975–1999 period continued to touch individual lives because most families lost a loved one during the invasion, the occupation or the militia rampage following the independence ballot.

The anniversary was also marked by the exchange of 'diplomatic notes' between Australia and Timor-Leste for the joint exploitation of the Greater Sunrise oil and gas fields in the Timor Sea, 450 kilometres north-west of Darwin. After protracted negotiations the permanent maritime boundary between the two nations was finally determined with the majority of revenues flowing to Dili. At a formal ratification ceremony at Timor's Government Palace, Prime Minister Scott Morrison conveyed Australia's praise for Timor-Leste's efforts in nation-building:

> Today you are a proud nation, a young nation, risen from the ashes. One that's shown the world how to overcome violence with peace and rebuild what was torn down. In just 20 years you have built a vibrant democracy; you've created the institutions that support it, and held the free and peaceful elections that sustain it. You've built hospitals and schools and roads. You've brought down infant mortality and poverty, and eradicated polio. You've travelled a long road, and I believe even more progress and prosperity lie ahead. I'm very proud that Australia is part of your journey.[4]

The prime minister announced that Australia would refurbish Timor-Leste's naval base at Hera on the north coast and help with developing high speed internet infrastructure (to replace expensive and unreliable satellite services). Australia's aid package was partly prompted by China's increasing ties with Australia's near neighbour.

Two days before Prime Minister Morrison's arrival, Timorese students and activists were protesting against the decision of the Australian Government to prosecute a former ASIS agent, known as 'Witness K', (and his lawyer, Bernard Collaery) who had revealed that Australia had spied on the Timor-Leste Government during negotiations over Greater Sunrise in 2004. An Australian freelance journalist, Sophie Raynor, who lived in Dili from 2017 to 2019, claimed that, despite Morrison's claims of Australia's 'great friendship' with Timor-Leste:

> The truth is ... far longer and more fraught than he'd have you believe. It's an unjust, manipulative and exploitative relationship characterised by Australia's greed and short-sightedness. And it's a truth Australia must wake up to, lest it suffocate in its own stories.[5]

This was unbalanced, prejudicial and partial reporting that overlooked the realities of international relations and the full extent of Australia's relations with Timor-Leste. Raynor did not mention the very substantial expenditure borne by Australia for the UNAMET and INTERFET deployments or the cost of sustaining the United Nations Transitional Administration in East Timor (UNTAET) which preceded independence in 2002. There was no recognition of Australia's aid—in funding or in kind—only condemnation of rapacious Australian governments. She seems surprised that Australia would pursue its national interests in its dealings with Timor-Leste, as it does with every nation. Did Raynor believe that Beijing was any less self-interested in its dealings with Dili? Was she aware that most regional governments have been levering the spectre of possible Chinese presence to coerce the Australian Government into increasing its aid budget or providing facilities that Canberra is not convinced advances the national interests of its neighbours? Raynor also failed to mention concerns about the growing tide of official corruption in East Timor (according to the country's own anti-corruption commission) and neglected to explain that the World Bank's 'Ease of Doing Business' table ranked Timor-Leste 178 out of 190 nations. It is one thing to blame Australia for the pursuit of national self-interest, it is another to excuse or excise from consideration the conduct of the East Timorese. The dynamics of any relationship are influenced by the character of all the participants. Spying on the Timorese was, of course, the wrong thing to do and they deserved better from Australia.

$$\bigstar\bigstar\bigstar\bigstar$$

Twenty years after INTERFET, several key individuals continue to influence the affairs of Indonesia, Timor-Leste and Australia. General Suharto died in January 2008 and, his successor, Dr BJ Habibie, in September 2019 (on the eve of the twentieth anniversary). General Wiranto, the head of the Indonesian military in 1998–1999, later served in several senior political roles and continued to exercise considerable personal influence over Indonesia's official attitude to the events of 1999. He was a member of President Joko Widodo's Cabinet when stabbed twice by a knife wielding Islamic extremist in October 2019. He later lost his Cabinet post but was appointed to the nine-member Presidential Advisory Council in December 2019.

In East Timor, at the time of writing, continuing political instability has led to the first president and former prime minister, Xanana Gusmão, returning to a national leadership position. Former president José Ramos-Horta remains an influential figure in East Timorese politics although his focus in recent years has turned to international crisis management. The militia leader, Eurico Guterres, was sentenced by an Indonesian special court to ten years in prison for his role in the post-ballot violence but was detained for less than two years after his conviction was overturned. He was politically active after his early release but exercises no enduring influence on either Indonesian or Timorese affairs. Joao Tavares, described by the United Nations as the 'supreme militia commander', was also indicted for war crimes but was never brought to trial. He started living at Atambua in sight of the Timor-Leste border in 2004 before dying of a stroke in June 2009.

And in Australia, the Coalition Government led by John Howard lost office and the prime minister his seat in parliament at the November 2007 election. He and his former foreign minister, Alexander Downer, continue to believe the liberation of East Timor was one of the Howard Government's foremost achievements. Former Major General Peter Cosgrove was later promoted to the ranks of Lieutenant General and then General, appointed Chief of the Army and subsequently Chief of the Defence Force, and became Governor-General and was knighted before retiring from public office in June 2019.

For Australians of my generation, East Timor remains a symbol of hope. Despite international indifference to their suffering and widespread disinterest in their desire for self-determination, the East Timorese refused to accept any of the conveniences flowing from Indonesian rule and never accepted the opinion of outsiders that they would be better served materially by their incorporation into the Indonesian republic. This is not what they wanted for themselves or their children. Largely through their own courage and strength, they eventually wore down the political resolve of Jakarta and helped Canberra to rediscover its conscience. Their campaign for freedom started in 1975 shortly after the South Vietnamese ended theirs. This remains the starkest contrast in the two long-running conflicts that spanned the first 40 years of my life. Australia's role in both is not without controversy as participants, observers and scholars still try to make sense of what happened and why. Their views differ—as they should given the validity of diverging interpretations. But they are united in wanting to draw enduring lessons and abiding insights that will inform public opinion and the political mood the next time Australia is confronted by the difficulty of deciding between principles and practicalities, in distinguishing what is politically necessary from what is morally right.

Endnotes

1   Richard Woolcott, 'Howard's 'noble' act was folly, *The Age*, 7 March 2003.
2   See https://www.abc.net.au/news/2019–08-29/declassified-us-intelligence-documents-sheds-light-timor-leste/11459284. A similar line was taken by Paul Daley writing in *The Guardian Australia*: https://www.theguardian.com/commentisfree/2019/aug/30/australia-cast-itself-as-the-hero-of-east-timor-but-it-was-us-military-might-that-got-troops-in
3   Clinton Fernandes, *Reluctant Saviour: Australia, Indonesia and the Independence of East Timor*, Scribe, Melbourne, 2004.
4   https://www.pm.gov.au/media/remarks-maritime-boundary-treaty-ceremony
5   Sophie Raynor, 'Australia's true relationship with Timor-Leste', *Eureka Street*, vol. 29, no. 18, 9 September 2019.

www.ingramcontent.com/pod-product-compliance
Lightning Source LLC
Chambersburg PA
CBHW060341100426
42812CB00003B/1075